Casting Quiet Waters

Casting
Quiet Waters

REFLECTIONS
ON LIFE AND FISHING

Edited by
Jake MacDonald

GREYSTONE BOOKS

Vancouver/Berkeley

Greystone Books Ltd.
www.greystonebooks.com

Cataloguing data available from Library and Archives Canada
ISBN 978-1-77164-024-4 (pbk.)
ISBN 978-1-77164-025-1 (epub)

Editing by Stephanie Fysh
Cover design by Jessica Sullivan and Nayeli Jimenez
Text design by Nayeli Jimenez
Cover photograph by iStockphoto.com
Printed and bound in Canada by Friesens
Distributed in the U.S. by Publishers Group West

We gratefully acknowledge the financial support of the
Canada Council for the Arts, the British Columbia Arts Council,
the Province of British Columbia through the Book Publishing
Tax Credit, and the Government of Canada through the
Canada Book Fund for our publishing activities.

Greystone Books is committed to reducing the consumption
of old-growth forests in the books it publishes.
This book is one step toward that goal.

Contents

Introduction

FISHING IS AN age-old subject. The ancient Egyptians fished with hook and line in the Nile, the Romans used feathered flies to catch trout in hillside streams, and the "fish story" has been around almost as long as humanity itself.

The first book about fishing was published more than five centuries ago by an English nun named Dame Juliana Berners. Her *Treatysse of Fyshynge wyth an Angle* (1488) gives advice on everything from rod construction to streamside behavior. And her advice on many of those subjects is still good today: *"Looke that ye shadowe not the water, for that wyll fraye the fyshe. And if a fysshe be a frayde: he wyll not byte long after."*

Over the years, uncountable thousands of fishing books have been published, ranging from how-to manuals and travel guides to memoirs and novels, so it's of little help to introduce this collection as "a fishing book." The concept arose in much the same way as one might decide to throw a dinner party—let's invite some of the most respected writers at work in their fields to contribute a fishing story. As you'll see, most of the authors decided to use the subject of fishing as an opportunity to pursue larger existential questions. This too continues the tradition that Dame Juliana established five centuries ago. Like her obscure treatise, this collection turned out to be as much about life as fishing.

Despite the comic reputation of the "fish story" and the common perception of anglers (and fiction writers) as helpless liars, readers may notice that very few of these stories are about "catching the big one." It's a curious fact that anglers (and writers) seem little interested in stories of success. When anglers (or writers) are gifted by exceptional good luck, they usually keep it quiet, unless asked. They might tentatively offer to show a photograph or hang the mounted trophy in some cubbyhole corner of the house where it will gather dust and not get looked at. This has less to do with modesty than with the essential values of the sport: fishing is not about winning—it's about striving. If Hemingway's Santiago hadn't persevered for eighty-four days without catching a fish, there wouldn't be a story, and we wouldn't have such compassion for him and for the great marlin that must die so Santiago can live. (At least he doesn't have to kill the moon.) Yet as every angler knows, fishing is a sport in which the odds ride with the house. And like Leonard Cohen's gambler, every angler is looking for "a card that is so high and wild he'll never need to deal another." Of course, the perfect card will never show up. Every romance will end, and every hero will die. But the angler continues arcing his line out across the water, knowing that the reward is not in the catching but in the fishing.

Writers, like anglers, are forever trying to capture the ineffable, so the fish story comes naturally. The process of trolling the subconscious with sentence and paragraph is not so different from towing a lure through the unknown world beneath the surface of a river or lake. Both angler and writer toss lines, chase shadows, and spend countless hours wondering what might happen if they tried a different trick. Of course, one shouldn't burden the process with so much philosophical import that it becomes just another chore. The late, great fishing author Roderick Haig-Brown, of Campbell River, British Columbia, was at various times in his life a logger, a soldier, a Royal Canadian Mountie, a university chancellor, and a magistrate—all serious and weighty professions—but he wasn't a fan of the solemnity and hot air that inflates so many fishing books, and when he was asked once why he had devoted so much of his life to fly-fishing, he said, "I've thought about that quite a bit, and I've decided that it was because I enjoyed it."

In a wilderness region of British Columbia there is now a mountain named after him; it serves as an enduring tribute to his two favorite pastimes, fishing and writing. Dame Juliana, being a lady of the cloth, took a slightly more religious view of the sport. But if by some trick of time and fiction she ever emerged from the misty forests alongside the Campbell River and strolled, rod in hand, with the hawk-nosed, pipe-smoking old magistrate to partake of a morning of salmon fishing, I'm sure Haig-Brown would smile and nod his assent to her cautionary words on the real purpose of both literature and fishing: *"Ye shal not use this crafty sporte for the encreasing and sparing of your mony, but pryncypally for your solace, and the helth of your body, and specially of your soule."*

—JAKE MACDONALD

Bimini

MARNI JACKSON

*This has been adapted and expanded from a story
that originally appeared in* Saturday Night *magazine*

FIFTY MILES FROM Florida, lying athwart the Gulf Stream, Bimini has always lived off the bounty of passing ships. Long before the big yachts arrived, the island was a Prohibition rumrunning base, and in the nineteenth century, the islanders salvaged what they could from the frequent shipwrecks on the reefs off the north shore. The pirate Blackbeard briefly made it his base in the eighteenth century. Now, golfers and gamblers head for Nassau, but the big-game fishermen all go to Bimini, the Atlantic capital of marlin fishing.

In the early thirties, Ernest Hemingway took a fancy to the island—a cluster of three, really, but North Bimini, seven miles long and "two blocks wide," is where most people live. "I liked it as well as any other place I've spent time in," he wrote. "Except for the sleek private yachts that come over from Miami, it might be situated at the end of the world." There is, of course, an End of the World saloon on Bimini, with blender drinks, a beach-sand floor, and a backgammon table that has dice so worn and faded only the locals can read them. Parts of *Islands in the Stream* were written here, where Hemingway stayed in room number one at the Compleat Angler, a combination inn, saloon, and library well marinated in time and dreams. The walls are teak and the tables are old rum kegs. It's also the site of a modest Hemingway shrine, with photographs of the writer standing on the dock beside a strung-up tuna slightly taller than him. He has a drink in one hand and his arm is wrapped around the fish like a proud bridegroom on his wedding day.

Hem was not a beloved figure on the island. (Hanging beside the trophy photo are the words to a local calypso song about the writer, entitled "Big Fat Slob.") When he got drunk, which was fairly often, he used to wander down late at night to Brown's marina in his bathrobe and try to machine-gun the sharks that swam in close to shore. He seemed to like shooting fish almost as much as catching them; on his first trip from Cuba to Bimini, he was firing at fish from the boat when he accidentally shot himself in the foot and had to turn back to the mainland for medical attention. There's an account of one Bimini fishing trip when he did catch a 514-pound tuna—not all that big, but remarkably intact (sharks often eat the catch before the boat gets back to shore). Hemingway celebrated, then went down to the weigh scales where the eleven-foot tuna was strung up and began to punch it like a punching bag.

The writer also staged impromptu boxing matches on the Bimini docks, offering $100 or $200 for any "big Negro" who could outbox him wearing six-ounce gloves. Even William Saunders, an islander rumored to have once carried a piano on his head, couldn't beat him.

Beside the marina is Brown's bar, a caboose-shaped room built right out over the ocean. The tropical light that filters through the bamboo blinds is so unreal it might as well be darkness, and the drinkers sit buoyed in this viscous light like fish in an aquarium. The wooden walls are covered in lacquered shark jaws and stuffed sailfish, with their hook wounds varnished over. There's a picture of someone with his face sticking out between two large naked breasts, alongside a signed photo of Sammy Davis Jr., and more shots of anglers posing with their trophy fish. Above the bar is a cartoon showing a bunch of customers rolling around on the floor in helpless laughter as the bartender says to someone who's just arrived, "You say you want it by when?"

It's a hot afternoon in August, and I'm waiting, like the others, for the fishing to be over and the boats to come in. It's the annual Bimini Native Fishing Tournament; 104 anglers are still out on the water, hoping for the Big One. In the meantime, Brown's bar is in its customary state of suspended animation.

A fifty-something blonde woman sits at the bar in her dry bathing suit, with a tattered paperback and her room keys in front of her. She has a slightly dilapidated face, a husky smoker's voice, and a peculiar dignity sitting there at the precise center of the bar, as if she knows that time is running out and she plans to meet it head on. Like the island itself, which a historian once called a "ruined princess," she makes you think of death and beauty at the same time—these Hemingway thoughts come easily on Bimini.

The door opens and Jimmy the bass player walks in. Tall, black, and completely bald, Jimmy wears a T-shirt with a map of Canada on it and the slogan "Where the hell is Winnipeg?" He whispers something to the woman at the bar, who throws her head back and laughs a fabulous laugh. This transaction has the effect of slowing down time, something the Bahamians do very well. Over in the corner is deep-sea diver Neal Watson, who once flew a gyrocopter between Miami and Bimini. Dick the Miami bailhunter sits beside me and orders a Goombay Smash. "I'd like to apologize for my cousin's behavior," he says, nodding toward a man slumped at the end of the bar who keeps weakly repeating the phrase "Let's party" to no one in particular.

Neville the bartender plays cards with a retired dentist in a Panama hat sucking on an unlit cigarette in an ivory holder. Neville, who wears his wiry hair in a little front-loaded pyramid called a Bop, will occasionally interrupt his game to swim up and down the length of the bar, dispensing drinks and saying little, a silence that takes on a moral quality. All the drinkers are thirsty for Neville's approval. Although Bimini is famous for its game fishing—a 1,069-pound marlin was caught here the previous summer—there are other deep waters here besides the Gulf

Stream that flows by it. Atlantis seekers still make pilgrimages here, to snorkel over the strikingly symmetrical rocks known as the Bimini Road, off the north shore of the island. (Party-pooping geologists insist that this is simply how the indigenous limestone beachrock behaves as it breaks down over time.) There have long been rumors of a Fountain of Youth (or at least a freshwater spring) in the mangrove swamps of East Bimini too.

None of this factors in the bales of marijuana that wash up on the north end of the island, or the whalers that make the crossing to Florida at night, carrying Haitians to the mainland for $700 a head. Women also come here to dance with the locals, who are less desperate to score than the retired Miami CEOs in their Hatteras yachts, grimly pursuing their pleasure. You don't have to sit long in Brown's bar to notice that everyone is fishing for one thing or another.

"I'N'T HE JUST the *ugliest* thing you've ever seen," says Angie, hooking her long blonde hair behind her ear to peer at the new addition to the bar's fish tank. It was a black bullfish, a morose species that looks like a toad and walks on its fins. "Holy smokes, you are the ugliest little fish." She drags a long fingernail down the side of the tank. There are some women who spend a portion of their lives either on a boat or in a bar, moving up and down the chain of six hundred islands between the two Americas, and Angie is one of these. Her boyfriend, Bobby, charters a game-fishing boat called *The Mr. Nice Guy*. Usually, Angie goes out with him, but "sometimes they get kinda funny about having a woman aboard," so today she's stayed on shore. Wearing a turquoise halter top and cut-off shorts, she lives in her tanned skin like it's a three-piece suit. Her arms and legs glint with a fine golden down that I imagine is some kind of evolutionary response to living in the sun and on the water, day after day. Angie drinks rum and seems slightly, becomingly drunk all the time. She also likes to fish. The previous year she caught a 519-pound white marlin—almost the same size as Hemingway's tuna, in fact.

"It took me five and a half hours of fighting on an eighty-pound test line," she drawls in her Texas accent, "and it nearly *killed* me. The next day, everything ached, my ass was sore, my feet hurt, I could hardly walk upstairs. My fish was fourteen feet long and I got the bill mounted up real nice with a silver cap on it."

So, how do you catch a fish like that, I asked.

"When you feel him take the line, you point the rod right at him, till you feel him *good,* then you pull back hard to set the hook. Physically, I could do it, but mentally it was *haaard,*" she says, making the word trisyllabic. "A white marlin in the hardest thing to keep on the hook—they're not as big as the blue, but they really jump. And when you catch them and they come up to the surface, they're all lit up blue."

But are women strong enough to haul in something that weighs that much? "I think a woman's a better angler. For one thing, she's dying to do it right, and she'll listen to what the captain tells her. A lot of it is teamwork."

IT WAS FOUR o'clock, time for the fishing to stop, so we went out to the end of Brown's dock to watch the boats file into the harbor. They ranged from small skiffs with two people and a cooler of Heineken on board to $2,900,000 Hatteras yachts with smoked-glass dinettes and broadloomed decks. Some have a second-story perch called a tuna tower, where the captain can steer and spot distant schools of fish. This throne in the sky also leaves no doubt as to who is in control. The boats have names like *The Hard Bargain, Sweet Bunny*, or *The Molester II,* and etiquette onboard ship, no matter how dinky the vessel, is strictly hierarchical: what the captain says, you do.

I was staying at the end of the dock on a cement "character boat" hired out to diving parties. I had renamed this vessel *The Tragic Jack,* in honor of its tense and wiry owner. Jack reminded me of a deeply tanned and aged Jack Russell terrier. He sat on the upper deck late into the night, waiting for his "gal Friday" to return. She had run off with an islander named Cody, and I had a hunch she wouldn't be back. I had to pass Jack on my way down below deck to my tiny room, with its gold shag carpet and a gold-veined mirror opposite the bed. "Down at the Angler, eh?" he'd say. "Well, you'll get tired of that soon enough." He waved a cigarette toward the island. "I like these people, but you can't turn your back on them." I seemed to be his only guest, and I slept well; a cement boat is great for stability.

Walking along the marina, where the white masts of the anchored boats slowly wipe the sky like metronomes, I watched the girlfriends down in the lurching galleys cutting the crusts off the lunch sandwiches and I figured I knew what was going on here. I knew that the number of blue marlin have been shrinking, mostly as a result of the Japanese longline commercial fishermen working the coast, but the sport fishermen weren't helping the situation. I had my preconceptions all arranged.

Late in the afternoon, the anglers began hoisting their catch up to the scales to be weighed. Dead, discarded barracuda littered the ocean floor at the end of the dock; the large ones can be poisonous to eat. The boats come back with all kinds of fish: permit, dolphinfish, sailfish, wahoo. Every fish caught earns points, with sharks and billfish worth the most—ten points a pound. A rather small, pared-down boat caught my eye as it motored into the harbor. The man standing up in the tuna tower actually looked as if he belonged there. As he came alongside the dock, I saw that he had a sea-battered face with sharp blue eyes, and that he faintly resembled a tuna himself, solid in the middle and tapered at both ends. The boat was the *Falcon v*, and the captain was the legendary Jimmy Albury, holder of the Bahamian record for blue marlin, and the only skipper on record to catch four seven-hundred-pound marlin in three days—2,800 pounds of fish. As he joined the lineup to weigh his catch, a medium-sized sailfish, I started taking pictures of him.

"You should have been here yesterday when we caught a six-hundred-pound blue," he said.

The sailfish was lowered onto the dock. I lifted the sail and saw that it was really a delicate membrane, like a bird's wing.

"The thing to remember about Jimmy is that he never raised a marlin for four years," said another island angler, Johnny Dudas. "And he once went thirty-two days without a single bite. But he stays out there."

That night, I went looking for him in the dining room of the Big Game Club to find out what sort of man catches marlin for a living.

DRESSED IN BLACK as usual—he's known as the "Johnny Cash of fishing" on the circuit—Albury was burying his baked potato in sour cream when I sat down with him, his angler, Ernie Swint, and Ernie's two teenaged sons. Pretty soon Albury was supplying me with fishing stories, but all about other people.

"Women are better anglers, in my opinion," he said. "They've got endurance. I remember this one gal, she was eighteen years old and weighed 165 pounds. At six feet tall, one hunk of a woman. She hooked a blue and fought it for ten and a half hours. Around dawn, lightning struck the leader and we lost the fish. She just bent over the rod and cried like a baby. But she put up one hell of a fight."

Jimmy was sixty-three when I met him, homely and sexy as a pirate. He wore his hair in a fifties' Elvis do, slicked back at the sides with a curl at the front. A Bahamian by birth,

Jimmy had moved to Miami with one of his five former wives. Around his neck he wore a Liz Taylor–worthy diamond on a fine gold chain. He stretched his arm across the table so I could take a close look at his ring, a little gold mermaid the size of a peach pit.

"She has diamonds in her hair, sapphires in her eyes, and rubies in her boobies," he said, and not for the first time. Like certain fish, the ring was not exactly pretty, but it was big. A trophy ring.

"Fishing's my profession," he explained, "but I also design jewelry and raise exhibition parakeets." If he wasn't wearing a shirt, he added, he'd show me his parakeet tattoo.

He and Ernie have fished together for years. When I asked what he did when he wasn't on the water, Ernie just said he was "in electronics." "Every time I come to see Jimmy, I like to bring him a tv." Albury collects Rolexes, gold coins, and televisions.

Jimmy said he was now happily living with his new partner, Nancy, who "got me out of a bad time back awhile." The two of them were waiting for Nancy to join them as they ordered desserts and Cutty Sarks.

Who's to stop you from cheating when you're out on the ocean with no one around for miles, I asked. How does that work?

"Cheating's easy to do," Jimmy says. "Whenever somebody catches a nine-hundred-pound Mako shark on a twenty-pound test line, you know something funny happened out there. There's a bunch of ways to make things easier. The captain can use the engine to sort of back into the fish. But for me that takes the fun out of it."

I was beginning to get the picture that fishing, even serious professional fishing, is largely about *not* fishing—or at least about not catching anything. It requires long intervals of focused waiting and Job-like patience. "I might not be a good fisherman, but I'm a hard fisherman," Albury told me. "Winning's nice, but it's just a fluke—a reward for attentiveness."

Although I didn't understand game fishing or much like the idea of "conquering" these great creatures for sport, I found myself warming to Jimmy and Ernie. They had humility. So far this was not a quality I had noticed among most of the anglers on Bimini, where the fish, the yachts, and the egos only come in two sizes: large and extra-large.

The next day was the final day of the tournament and my last chance to get out on a boat, but the *Falcon v* was too small to take on another crew member. I figured Angie could fix me up with a captain, and at this time of night I knew where I could find her—lifting her hair off the back of her neck on the dance floor of the Angler.

I started down Bimini's one dark road; the night was moonless, and the air was warm. A languid figure stepped out of the shadows, stood in front of me, and asked my name. He was probably from Nassau, where the night scene is a little more brazen than on Bimini, which still has a small-town feel. Failing to execute a detour, I summoned up my crabbiest Canadian voice and said, "What's *your* name?"

"Velvet," he said, circling my wrists with his hands. And what was I out so late looking for, he wondered. Well, Velvet, I said, I am just trying to find some club soda, which is really hard to come by on the island. Same thing with fresh vegetables, I continued, or even a nice cold can of V8 juice. Had he ever tried V8? Velvet quickly melted back into the night and I turned up the lane to the Angler.

Calypso music drifted out the screen door of the hotel into the little courtyard, where some local boys were sitting on the stone wall. One of them was telling a long, complicated joke about the Chinese running the world, which gave me the pleasure of hearing a Bahamian man imitate a Chinese person speaking English. I envied their beautiful, time-slowing laughter. They recapped the joke for me, finding it even more hilarious this time around. The night air was almost too sweet to abandon, but I followed the music up into the crowded room of dancers. An islander called Spider-man was doing his specialty, dancing on his hands.

I spotted Angie right away, her body adroitly orbiting the axis of the wineglass in her hand. I told her I was looking to go out on a tournament boat, and she pulled me over to one of the mates of the *Molester 11*, who consulted with his captain. "As long as you can stay out of the way and follow orders," he shouted to me over the music, "you can come along."

I'm your man, I said.

The next morning I presented myself at the side of a thirty-seven-foot Enterprise captained by John Dudas, the man I'd talked to about Albury the day before. He had blinding white teeth and looked like a lost Kennedy brother. I leaped the perilous little gap between dock and boat, and we motored through the tricky bottleneck that funnels out of the harbor into the wide navy lane of the Gulf Stream.

I climbed up to the bridge where Captain John was steering.

"Shouldn't be too rough out there today," he said, glancing sideways. "You don't get seasick, do you?" I told him that escalators, punts, rafts, and even driving through spring runoff make me sick, but that today would be different. It was all a matter of attitude.

Good girl, he said, as he radioed the tournament headquarters to let them know that the *Molester II* was ready to fish.

Noticing that the roll of the boat was worse higher up, I retreated below to the cabin, where the two mates, Bob and Quentin, were hooking baitfish called ballyhoo onto the four fishing lines. This involved squeezing the black liquid innards out of the fish's anal vent then sliding a metal rod through the fish's slim body and attaching it to a beaded chain to create a "flexible and natural running bait." The angler, a Miami attorney named Frank, was already installed in the fighting chair, where he sat like a sunburnt Poseidon, waiting for a strike.

The fighting chair is a lordly dais bolted into the stern deck of the boat. On the *Molester II*, the chair is flanked with four reels of shining brass that feed the lines out into the water. Two lines are threaded up through long poles called outriggers; this keeps the bait running close to the surface of the water and prevents the lines from tangling. "Clothespins," or taglines on the outrigger lines, snap off at the smallest tug, letting the crew know when a fish is toying with the bait.

When a strike comes, the crew jams the rod in play into a fixed holster that is mounted between the angler's legs. The other rods are slung back into the cabin and the angler gets down to work, leaning forward and rocking back, trying to keep the line taut, playing the fish until it tires—the customary phrase for this is "conquering the fish." This could take five minutes, or eight hours, until the angler can reel it in close to the boat. Then one mate gaffes it up on deck, where the other mate wields the simple little club known as the killing stick. Although the angler is the one who enjoys the Mycenaean splendor of the fighting chair, anyone—captain, mate, or fisherman—can lose the fish with one wrong move.

We were out in open water with the wind snatching off the tops of the waves. I was now horizontal in the cabin, awash in nausea. Beside me, the angler's girlfriend, Carol, was filing her nails. She was a real estate broker from Hollywood, Florida, and as the angle of the sun shifted, she changed her bikinis to vary the tan lines. Meanwhile, the two mates silently stared out over the water.

"The captain doesn't like any small talk while we're fishing," she whispered. "After all, there's money at stake." Not just the $30,000 Calcutta Division prize money, but the $500 to $600 a day it costs to charter the captain and stock the boat.

And as Hemingway wrote in *The Old Man and the Sea*, "it was considered a virtue not to talk unnecessarily at sea."

Carol was very nice to me, showing me pictures of her Maltese terrier Billy. Game fishing can be a lot of fun, she maintained, "but I still can't get used to the killing. It's just so obvious when they fight that the fish want to *live*."

By now some gyroscope had spun off balance in my head; I fought nausea, and tried to pretend I was the yellow bubble in a carpenter's level. As Carol made roast beef sandwiches for lunch, I turned away. She took a sandwich out to Frank, who said, "I only want half" and waved her off. She came back into the cabin, rolling her eyes for my benefit, and dug a cold can of Pepsi out of the cooler. When she brought him the half sandwich on a plate, Frank took his chewing gum out and put it on the end of her nose. "Cut it out," she said, but smiling. Then the first strike came.

"Woman, hold that chair!" one of the mates shouted to Carol, whose job was to keep the chair from swiveling too widely. The boat's engines roared to life and a mate hurled the extra rods into the cabin.

"It feels like a big one," said Frank as the line spun out. I cowered in the cabin, unable to lift my head above the horizon line. My official job was to slap the killing stick, scalpel-style, into the palm of the mate when he asked for it. The stick was small and heavy.

Then, as quickly as the excitement had begun, it ended; the hoped-for marlin turned out to be a twenty-one-pound dolphinfish, flashing pink and gold as it landed onto the deck. The mate took the stick from me, killed it neatly, and tossed it into a locker. They might eat it later; dolphinfish are especially good.

The lines were baited again, the engines cut back to a low gargle, and Carol went back to painting her nails. If only the *Molester II* were made out of cement like the *Tragic Jack*, I thought, grateful that this final tournament day would end early, at one p.m. Then another fish struck, the engines fired up, and Frank shouted, "It's a sail!" I looked up in time to see the heart-stopping arc of a silver-blue sailfish, standing out of the water like a seahorse. Carol rushed to her station behind the chair and I tried to focus my camera. This time the fighting lasted longer, and when the forty-pound sailfish was gaffed on board, I saw it light up briefly. Hemingway described it as a "colour almost like the backing of a mirror."

But this one seemed to have baby sailfish either inside it or somehow attached to it, and a gush of grayish-pink tadpoles poured across the deck.

"Oh, put those little bitty ones back," cried Carol, but nobody responded. When the mates rinsed the blood off the deck, the tadpoles were washed overboard anyway. Then the killing was done, and Carol went up to the bridge to round off her tan before we headed back to shore. I put my camera away.

The signal came over the radio that the tournament was officially over. Frank vaulted out of the chair and changed from a silent fish-killer back to an attorney out for a pleasure cruise. He snapped open another Pepsi and took his bad luck graciously. With indescribable relief, I noticed that we had turned in the direction of Bimini. But my relief was premature; black smoke began to issue from under the couch I was lying on, which brought the captain rushing down from the bridge.

"Excuse me just one sec," he said as I wobbled to another corner. He opened the engine housing and thick smoke poured out. The fan belt was burning up. The *Molester II* had to anchor a tantalizing two hundred yards from South Bimini while the mates worked on the engine.

If it was all the same to them, I announced, I was going to swim in circles around the boat until the problem was solved. I dove in and wondered how water could make you feel so bad on top of it and so good when you were in it. By the time the engine was restored and we came ashore, the crowds around the weigh stations had dispersed. Soon the sharks would come in to feed on the discarded barracuda, their dark shapes cutting through the water with reined-in rapacity.

That night, Jimmy Albury won the Calcutta Division and broke his own record, set four years earlier. He danced with Nancy like a young man in love, and I got to see the parakeet tattoo on his arm. Everyone ended up on the Angler dance floor, where a dental student from Maryland galloped me round the room, and then an islander led me through a proper merengue.

On my way back to the *Tragic Jack* I stopped to visit Michelangelo, a regular visitor to Bimini for the past forty years. A robust paraplegic who lives in his boat for much of the year, Michelangelo paints in oils and has a good collection of operas on tape. His wheelchair sat on the dock beside his boat, although sometimes he had to wait for the tide to come in before he could get from one to the other.

It was two a.m. and the sound of partying on the big yachts anchored offshore carried across the water. Michelangelo asked, would I care for some pasta? Or perhaps some Colombian?

At the end of the dock the captain of the *Tragic Jack* was still up, staring out toward the ocean, wondering where his girl had gone.

Trails of Tarpon

THOMAS MCGUANE

RUNNING DOWN THE sound in the dark, a three-quarter moon shining overhead and lighting a great path across the water, I pictured myself colliding with unlighted pilings, stone crab traps, or oyster bars that I couldn't see. Chains of islands to the east and west were just streaks in the night sky. I hoped I would recognize my destination, a small basin appended to a forked channel, when I got to it. There would be a row of fishermen's shacks on an oyster reef, an opening, then the resumption of the shallow bar. I knew I'd see the silhouettes of the shacks, but I was not so sure I'd see the opening. Indeed, I overran it, and only sudden dark shapes in front of me told me that I was about to go high and dry in a planing skiff, possibly wrecking the motor. By the time I shut down, I was floating in less than a foot of water. I got out my push pole and began to work my way in the presumed direction of the basin. If I had fetched up on some wide shallow, I would find no tarpon today. Fish were shooting off around me—redfish, I guessed—and it was interesting going, but uncertainty had taken away some of the pleasure. Then, at about the time I thought I would try a new angle, I pushed on until the pole dropped out from under me and I knew I was in the basin. I was confident that when the sun came up I'd be in the middle of a lot of innocent tarpon. If there were rollers, I'd see them in the moonlight or at daybreak, which was now less than an hour away. In any case, a bonanza was at hand. All I needed was a little light.

The sun came up, and I poled myself into an irritable sweat before admitting that the fish were not here. I was in the wrong place at the wrong time. I suppose if you can't take *this*, you can't take tarpon fishing. Only the vision of things going right, of fish this big that can run this far and jump this high, keeps tarpon fishermen knocking their heads against the mysteries. I had been immersed since the earliest fish showed in March, and despite some irregular success, I could think of little else. But the fuel bills were mounting, as miles by the thousands accumulated on the log of my GPS.

THERE IS A hidden bay, five miles to the east of my dock, where tidal creeks enter, ridged with oyster bars that form a kind of corset at its middle, dividing it into two sub-basins attractive to tarpon. They should be there—they've always been there—but they're not there now. Each morning I run to the basin in the dark, to the unearthly music of awakening waterbirds. It's hard to believe that anything in South Florida could be this remote. Before the morning breezes from the east or the later sea breeze from the west, the basins lie as mirrors of saltwater, marred only by the frivolous jumps of mullet or the deep pulling V of a hungry redfish. If the tide is low, I'll look for snook at first light, and I have often seen them emboldened by the hour, sometimes racing between the legs of wading birds in pursuit of mojarra minnows, glass minnows, and gobies. There is something funny about this, the tolerant birds trying to feed while the self-absorbed snook swim among their legs and shower them with their feeding rushes.

But this is about tarpon. When I've found them in years past, the fishing has had a classic quality: laid-up fish, floating, asleep but ready to be drawn into pursuit. This is exacting, addictive fishing; the casts must be accurate but from a distance. When the cast is right, and the fish stirs to track the fly, in all his great weight and pent-up exuberance, the excitement, the nearness to success, feels like fear. This year, I can't find them. The fish are not in short supply in nearby water—thick, even—but they're not coming *here*, not many, anyway, not enough. But on each visit something happens that makes me come back for another look. It's a free jumper rocketing from the water, hanging in midair before the crash that seems to be the fish's object; or it is a fish feeding, perhaps on a mullet; once, it is an abrupt canyon in the tannic water that closes, overlapping waves gathering at the middle of a subsiding hole, gone. I come back that night, the next morning; I never catch them. This is the scene of subtle opportunity, and I seem not to be up to it. At night as I drift off, I picture a sustained time during which I stay in those coupled basins, risking time-consuming failure until I understand tide, wind, and migration. Of course, if I succeed, it will be all mine and perhaps I will be slow to share my secret.

At the lower basin, jacks marauded along the mangroves with their backs out of the water, a scattered front of stormtroopers killing and eating on the run. I made a cast, but before it landed, they settled and disappeared: they're not dumb. In fact, in this shallow water, not much is dumb.

Along the mangroves, a pair of dolphins hunted snook and redfish, and their predatory surges sent shockwaves well down the shore. This is a much different picture of dolphins from the rolling, gamboling creatures we usually see; this is full of purpose, the controlled violence inescapable. Dolphins are, with sharks, a principal enemy of tarpon.

The sun was well up now, and the occasional boat appeared, probably fishing with popping corks for speckled trout. I have a collection of these popping corks that I've dug out of the mangroves, prettily weathered, some with rattles inside. These join my collections of battered white plastic buckets, which serve as the local fisherman's portmanteau, and of weathered net floats, all of which should be thrown away as they appear to others to be "crap." The howl of a rental boat going up on an oyster bar reminded me that I should be elsewhere if I hoped to catch a tarpon.

I had started the engine, and was idling while I thought about what to do when I received one of the gifts that come to anglers only when they fish unstintingly, especially in salt-water, where tide goes from something you read from a tide chart and memorize to something in your blood, a tissue laid over intuitions of fish movement, especially migra-tory movement, teased about by the vagaries of weather, by winds that change water temperature or produce lees in spe-cific places—from all of which comes the gift: a hunch.

Here was the hunch: a long grassy hump, almost black, in four feet of water with a round sand spot in the middle that would illuminate anything swimming over it. The fall-ing tide crossed it at an acute angle. It would be an ideal checkpoint for tarpon moving on the tide to one of the three passes that open to the Gulf of Mexico.

An angler who ignores his hunches discounts his oppor-tunities by half. This one was strong, and I followed it, a long run in a steep quartering chop that kept me in sting-ing spray until I entered the quieter waters of the sound. When I reached my spot, the hunch transformed itself into real conviction as I savored the light on my pass point, light that seemed to illuminate a broad area of turtle grass and the nicely defined edge. I anchored my skiff and tied the rod off with a quick-release knot, its bitter end attached to an orange float from my crap collection.

I was not long awaiting my travelers. First came a string of smaller fish, rolling merrily and a bit out of range. They were followed by singles and other strings of fish, also out of range. Then, just as my conviction began to weaken and I thought of moving my anchor, five big fish cut across the grass toward the edge from an entirely new angle, one less advantageous to me—it would have my fly approaching them from behind, something tarpon will not tolerate. I suspected that there might be one more fish, though, coming after these five. I cast just behind the last fish I could see and let my fly float until an apparition appeared, moving over the grass, and I started my retrieve. The fish moved so quickly, I never saw it. Instead, the rod jolted in my hand, the fish was running, and I was clambering to the stern to pull the slip-knot on my anchor line. The first jump was a twister that had the fish landing on its back; then one marlin-style with a lot of horizontal distance covered; then several more until they became diminished efforts, only the upper part of the fish's body breaking the surface. Still, I had trouble moving it and had to go to the fish with the motor. I stopped and tried to turn the fish, which responded with shorter and shorter but still powerful surges. We had gone a long way together, halfway across the sound. The tarpon was finning beside the boat now. The lower jaw makes a good grip for removing the hook, and I held on for a few more moments just to feel its weight, its remaining power.

The best part of fishing is watching a fish swim away, in no particular hurry. Now to hunt up the orange float, and perhaps have my beer and my ham sandwich. It was ninety degrees out, and I was imagining the big chunk of ice in my cooler, the lovely breeze as I ran home.

I WENT OUT to the Gulf on a hot June evening to fish one tide. It was quiet, just a few swimmers on the beach in the distance and towering pink, dark-bellied thunderheads over the mainland. I scared some tarpon as I maneuvered into my stakeout and was not waiting long before the first fish came along from the south—singles, pairs, strings, all moving quickly. I misunderstood the speed of the first fish; they overtook me before I could present my fly and flushed from the boat in whirlpools of turbulence. The next bunch came at a bad angle to my left, but I cast anyway, and to my surprise, the biggest fish turned out and tracked my fly for a long way then lifted up in the deep shoveling take that no one gets accustomed to, and I hooked it. This, like most first jumps, seemed enraged, an attempt to knock me out with the first blow. Then came several more blows just as violent, followed by a burning run. The fight took us straight offshore in fading light. Trying to force the issue, I leaned into the 11-weight, faithful friend of over a decade, and broke it. The shattered tip traveled down the backing, the sharp edge of the broken butt cut the backing, and my fly line went over the horizon. If there is any weakness in your tackle, tarpon find out about it.

A FRIEND, A guide, was in my living room with the battered insulated coffee cup with which guides keep their bodies in motion during tarpon season. He looked discouraged. "I had my guy in fish all day. Nice guy. But stupid. IQ around 55, but we got along great. Show him a hundred fish and he goes, 'Which one do I cast to?' He casts and I have to tell him to strip. 'Strip,' I tell him. '*STRIP! STRIP! STRIP!*' It was hopeless. At the end of the day, still no fish. He asks me to tell him what he should do. I'm like, 'Dude! I can't take any more! Catch a tarpon! *I recommend that you catch a tarpon.*'"

Other friends show up, most with beer in hand. We have line burns in the crevices of our fingers. There are bits of eighty-pound fluorocarbon in the rug from building shock tippets. An argument breaks out as to whether the Slim Beauty knot is as a strong as the Australian Plait or the Bimini Twist. Everyone is thinner than they were sixty days ago. Two-stroke engines have made us half deaf. We try to remember the last time we read a book or newspaper. One sport says the president was flying to France to meet with a bunch of cheese-eating surrender monkeys. The fishing guides seem embittered that when they finally get into fish, the clients have to go back for massages or manicures. There is some tension between the guides and us unguided "privateers."

One guide who naps at my house started his day at five in the morning, took a short nap at midday, fished till nine at night, dropped the client, headed out to fish himself, came in at 3:30 a.m., made a peanut butter and jelly sandwich in my kitchen, and picked up his clients ninety minutes later for another day on the water. Some guides actually like to fish.

I really should catch up on the news. Here and there, we are advised to stay the course. Tests show that doctors' ties are full of germs. Most Americans are too busy to floss.

Others have made "the ultimate sacrifice." Everything on the news seems so abstract, especially the pompous overviews of the talking heads. The fishing has become a parallel universe. It can't last, can it? Probably it shouldn't, but it seems so real next to the streaming nightmare on the news. Still, it's not right either to lament that you can fish only when you are awake—nothing realistic about that. I can get pretty abstract myself, too, explaining that I'm "trying to get to the bottom of this" by way of accounting for how it got so out of control for three unbroken months.

"When do you think you're coming home?" asked my wife.

"I have a ticket for Sunday," I assured her.

"Do you think you'll be on that plane?"

After a thoughtful pause, I said, "I wish I knew." I said that I was like the house cat that had been making love to a skunk.

"How's that, dear?"

"I haven't had enough but I've had all I can stand."

"Ha ha," she said mirthlessly. "I think you can stand more. Yes, I think you can stand more. Have you learned anything?"

"I've learned that you cannot live entirely on Krispy Kreme doughnuts."

"Oh."

"You must have fiber. By combining Krispy Kremes with Metamucil and black coffee, I have a complete diet."

I'd actually had a nice evening meal sitting on my poling platform in the rolling Gulf, where I looked for fish, rod in reach. I'd laid out cold sliced pineapple, slices of Fuji apples, a big piece of Black Diamond cheddar, a wedge of cold

31

sirloin, and a green-glass bottle of beer. Sometimes I saw a manta ray jump, or a manatee bulge to the surface, or a shoal of bait go airborne, or frigate birds sortie forth on a twilight mission, the heedless plunges of pelicans, a sail on the horizon... It was quite good. Yes, a pleasant way to dine. I had been less pleased in the smoky twilight of famous French restaurants.

Then, where the Pass met the deep flat, where the color changed from cobalt to foamy mid-Gulf pale green, right there, a string of playful tarpon was streaming north, the late light illuminating the frolic and the long bar of silver when several rolled at once. It was my job now to guess where they were going, to get there and shut down quietly. The line of travel was constant, and I had little difficulty moving into their path to wait. I began checking my equipment more urgently as the fish approached—checked the line, checked the loop in the water for flotsam of any kind, the fish now with separate bodies and those curiously unseeing above-the-water eyes. Every few seconds a tail kicked clear as a fish fed, then they started to chain up, straightened again, and came my way. I looked once more to see if I was standing on line then threw my reading glasses around behind my back on their lanyard. I had suddenly remembered how they've snagged line and robbed me of fish before. Now I began talking to myself: *They're not in range, they're not in range, please be cool.* The lead fish was bigger than the others, dorsal slicing the water and pulling a quarter wave behind him. These fish were going *fast.* As they bore off slightly to my left, I cast an interception, waited, then retrieved across the vision of the lead fish. Instead of taking the fly as it crossed in front of him, the fish slowed and began to track it, for twenty feet, until I was thinking we were within a couple of yards of the boat flushing the whole school. But the fish pushed up behind my fly, tilted, and that stupendous maw opened, and my fly went down. I continued to strip until I had contact, then, using only my stripping hand, I struck the fish and tightened, reaching with my line hand as far away from my side as I could. The coils were leaping toward the stripping guide and then I was clear, and in the words of Mike Tyson, "It's on."

The first jump often seems to express the greatest fury: the olive-brown fish in the water has become the plated silver fish in the air; his body curving violently, and again, he reaches for the sky. The reentry is a heedless crash, then a reorientation into a straightaway dash, the substantial line becoming the seemingly insubstantial backing when the run accelerates and I feel the elevation of line as another jump and another, each crazier than the last, marks several spots in the sea at once.

Why is it so thrilling? Why is it *incomparably* thrilling? It's the contest joined, but it's also a kind of euphoric admiration and—this is risky—it feels like love. You watch your fish and you are filled with admiration, transported by beauty. Isn't that love? It was in high school!

The jumping has proven costly and the fish must now slug it out with you and you don't necessarily want to slug it out with him. Barring tackle failure, you have every chance of winning this phase, but make it quick: learn every fish-fighting technique out there, because love and admiration are not the same as beating up the object of your desire. I have become ambivalent about this side of angling. I delight in seducing fish, at insinuating myself into their private world, but defeating fish has less appeal—though I continue to boat tarpon from time to time, to remind us both that this is mortal combat. There comes a moment when your silver paladin is once again the brown and somewhat humbled but still potent fish that took your fly. But when he stands off at half the length of your line and tries to roll in exhaustion, it is time to quickly boat him and remove your fly or to break him off.

BY LATE MAY, a tarpon-fishing death march was in play. George was napping between sessions on a rolled-up tarp in my carport. Montana log builder Bill Hart tried sleeping on the porch, but soaking with sweat, adjourned to the dock, where he rested on the widely spaced planks. Austin snoozed in the guest room. Crushed ice in the coolers didn't make it through the day, and we turned to blocks. Three guys and a Gordon setter from West Yellowstone never came ashore. It was part of the Montana hatch on the Gulf. My charge account at the fuel dock kept me at arm's length from reality, and we all fingered places on our bodies to speed up the dialogue with our dermatologists. Predawn runs were at fatalistically high RPMs; the imagination that once conjured up hazards now only pictured the destination and its fish. The tarpon came in pulses from the south and we watched for them like herons with the hope that our trails would cross on the pale green Gulf of Mexico.

A few times, when a hunch placed me in some incongruous spot—a breach in the mangroves, the corner of a tidal bore—the tarpon appeared, for just long enough for me to think "There you are!" as the fish changed direction and swam out of range. A moment of recognition between two watchful beasts.

We like to think that we know things while animals are merely programmed. Tarpon know to spawn offshore, and their progeny know to head inshore to the brackish mangroves to grow up safely. They know to follow migrating baitfish, and they know at what stage of tide the crabs hatch. They know to go south in the spring and up rivers when it's cold, and when to return south in the fall. Some know their way around both coasts of Florida and the Gulf to Louisiana and Texas. They know which fish they can eat and which ones can eat them. They know man is a bad thing the first time they see him. They know when the polalo worm hatches and will travel for miles to arrive just as dinner is served. They know that a safe snooze can be had in the shade of a Gulfport or Key West shrimp trawler. By the time you can catch tarpon consistently, when you are convinced you know what they know, you think so much like them that your affection can create problems.

GEORGE AND MARSHALL and I were fishing one May evening on a long, sweet, curving shoreline that seemed to be a runway for inbound tarpon traffic. The fish were assembling in loose groups then stringing out in meandering lines, happy fish with one thing in common: they weren't biting. We threw everything at them, but they weren't even courteous enough to boil off in indignation. Each had that faraway look that is connected less to hunger than to destiny. This produces a new kind of effort from the angler: narcissistic casting based on no expectation of results. Tight loops! Casts so long no hook could be set! Another string of travelers came by, all average fish. I cast, and from the shadows beneath the string, a very different fish arose and wolfed my fly. I set the hook, and the fish jumped with magnificent hang time. "That's a big fish," George stated. Marshall said, "Tom, that's an awful big fish." The hook was firmly set, the fish began that run characteristic of big tarpon—reminiscent of expensive German automobiles—and *ping!* The reel froze. The three of us looked into the reel's arbor. I was sad and shaken.

"What was that all about?"

"What happened?"

"Could I have done something?"

"A trapped loop?"

"The reel malfunctioned. I wish I was dead."

"There'll be more."

"Like that?"

"Well ..."

"Like *that?*"

The next day, things began going haywire for everybody. I put a lot of pressure on a straight-running, non-jumping fish, the Dacron backing stripped the coating off my fly line at the nail knot, and the fly line was gone with the leader fly and the fish. George reported that loose fly line jumping around the deck while a tarpon ran caught the keys to his boat, ripped them out of the ignition, and threw them overboard. I had just taken an early-morning jaunt with George, who believes that when it comes to a fast skiff, you should "drive it like you stole it." Indeed, while we hurtled along, I took a concerned look at the GPS to get a real idea of our speed. As we whined and skittered south toward Fort Myers, I determined we were pushing sixty and that not much of the boat was ever actually in the water. "The reason this thing is so slow," George explained, noting my alarmed stare at the speed indicator, "is I have the wrong prop on it."

I ADMIRED THE sunset, a fabulous peach meringue with towering thunderheads straight out of the Arabian Nights. It wasn't long before tarpon began to appear, pushing uptide in long strings. This was going to be perfect. I turned the boat around bow to the tide and anchored, then attached my buoy with a quick-release knot. Not long after, I was up on the bow, line stripped out and ready, I could see fish rolling on an undeviating course, and my heart began to pound.

A running guide boat slowed just offshore of me to see what I was doing. I hoped the tarpon wouldn't roll again, but they did and the guide started his electric motor and moved up an eighth of a mile to cut me off. My day was over. The guides' version is: We're trying to make a living. The privateers' version is: They're pimping our wildlife. I went back to the house to watch the Calgary Flames in the semifinals. The ice looked good, especially right after the Zamboni, when all is well with the world and the good air rises from the rink.

Once June came around it was hot before the sun came up. Standing on the deck fueling my skiff, I could watch my sweat rain around my feet. Idling out of the canal, my eyes went to patches of shade and not to the glare of the Gulf beyond. Instead of thinking how many trout it would take to make a meal for a tarpon, I began to think how beautiful a trout looks when it tips up under a mayfly. And what about a nice cow in a green meadow? The tropics make a man forget reading, writing, and arithmetic, which my checkbook could confirm. How clever folks are in the north, I marveled. The local hotel's shutting down whole wings was grimly logical; the rapidly decaying local civility gave rise to an ill-tempered poetry as angry folks tried to communicate. At the store, the oranges were from California, the mangoes from Brazil, and the berries from Chile. The bag boy, age eighty, was from Yonkers; the checkout clerk, Cleveland. The entire island was covered with green, rapidly growing plants advancing on seasonal homes with ill-concealed malice.

I hooked a hot fish on the edge of the Intracoastal Waterway. When it went airborne, a cigarette boat full of bathing beauties stopped to watch but left in a roar when the tarpon stopped jumping. Then I was alone with the fish. After two long, straight runs, it let me bring it slowly to the boat. My arms were dead. I hung over the gunwale and removed the fly, then held the great fish by its lower jaw. I could see every detail of its iridescent shape in the pellucid green water, turtle grass and seashells a few feet below. The slow beat of its tail pulsed all the way up through my shoulder, even into my body; its lazy power curled the water. I hung low over the side of the boat until I looked straight into those huge black eyes. I said, "I gotta go." I opened my hand and all the migratory wisdom in that gaze faded to green and the fish was gone. I knew I'd make that plane.

The Trophy Wall

BY CHARLES WILKINS

UNTIL I WAS eight or nine, I had never tasted a freshwater fish other than the bejeweled sunfish that we harvested by the dozens within fifty feet of the cabin dock on Clear Lake, at Torrance, Ontario. We baited our hooks with worms that we had bought at Charlie Tong's store and had cut into such tiny fragments that a single earthworm could get my sisters and me through an hour or more of brisk action. One time my mother, an all-but-heroic small-timer where fishing was concerned, found a fat half-worm in the stomach of one of the fish she was cleaning by the back door. After reminding me gently that worms cost 20 cents a dozen (which at the time would have equaled my allowance for a week), she threw the slightly digested fragment back into the bait can and covered it with moss for the next day's outing.

I had a child's interest in maps, and have recalled many times over the years that when these pungent small-fry—gutted, headless, and scaled—went into the frying pan, they were shaped like South America. By the time they came out, drastically foreshortened by the heat, they had become Africa and had taken on an appetizing crustiness that belied their questionable status as food. Between episodes of getting the bones caught briefly in our throats (which, happily, occurred no more than once or twice a sitting and could be solved by swallowing dry bread), we enjoyed every pinch of the sweet bluish flesh that, with effort, could be chewed from each fish's tiny flanks.

It was not so much the eating, of course, as the catching that made small-fry worth the effort. Not long ago, an old friend, a skilled and veteran angler, summed up the joys of "going small" by explaining to me that, in all his years of landing muskie, salmon, dorado, char, bonefish, sturgeon, etc., on all of the continent's finest fishing waters, his purest thrill as an angler had been leaning over the dock as a six- or seven-year-old with a few feet of string on a stick or around his hand, a grasshopper on his hook, and a kid's sense of anticipation as a few fingerlings or rock bass were drawn inexorably toward the bait. And, of course, took it, thus initiating his lifelong pleasure in the tug at the other end of the line, with its mysterious intimations of "down there," the measured reeling or lifting, and the possession or release of the prize.

Once or twice a summer, my sisters and I—or sometimes my dad or a visiting relative—experienced the thrill of hooking a catfish or perch. But our hope of catching something sportier was as futile, to use Margaret Atwood's phrase, as "enticing whales with a bent pin."

All of which is why, on an evening in late July, nearly fifty years ago, when my dad landed a twenty-two-inch smallmouth in front of the family cabin, my stupefied mother, having gutted and beheaded the beast, decided that some sort of record of it should be preserved for posterity. Lacking a camera, she traced the headless carcass onto the back of an unfolded Kellogg's Rice Krispies box, cut it out, and wrote on the tracing in thick black marker, "Caught by Hume on half a rubber worm, at dusk, July 27, 1966."

Half a rubber worm! Cue the fishing gods, who alone know that only my mother, a sweet, rural child of the Depression, could have invested this ludicrous revelation with the same level of pride as anyone else might have experienced had their fish been caught on a monster Mepps or galloping Rapala and mounted on varnished oak.

At the bottom, along the cutout's belly, she added the word "cleaned," as if to dispel any suspicion that headless lunkers might be loitering in the depths of Clear Lake.

Lacking a convenient place to display the cutout, she taped it to the paneling above the west bedroom door. It wasn't long before it attracted other cutouts, mostly on cereal-box cardboard—a collection that we eventually began referring to as the Fish Wall or Trophy Wall.

The smallest of these formidable likenesses depicts a five-inch rock bass, the first catch of my first child, Matthew, in perhaps 1993, while the others comprise an erratic natural history of the creatures of Clear Lake: whiskery catfish, obese sunfish, puny perch, a nine-inch crappy, the skinniest pike ever (a fish whose tracing suggests a garter snake with fins). The most exotic of the cutouts recalls a seven-inch crayfish that at age three my daughter Georgia plucked off the lake bottom, dead and well tenderized by decomp, and offered to me, thinking I would want to barbecue it. When I did not, she settled for having it memorialized on the Trophy Wall.

The whole piscine farce would hardly be worth mentioning except that over the years it has become for me a kind of cartoon tracery of family preferences and protocol, a reminder not just of my parents' unassuming and unselfconscious ways but of the fact that among all the fishermen I have known, met, or observed during more than six decades on the planet, we the Wilkinses possess, unquestionably, the lowest standards, the faintest expectations, and the slimmest expertise. From our lowly perch, we perhaps also hold the greatest potential for joy in catching anything at all that might, on occasion, sink its teeth into our half rubber worm.

The wall is equally a reminder of the relentless and inescapable flux in which every living creature plays a part. Some of the represented species are long gone from the lake, some of the fishermen long gone from the planet.

Among the ranking absentees is my dad, Hume Wilkins, a man who late in his life, when I asked him what he thought about while he was fishing (he spent hours in a frail fiberglass punt in front of the cabin, catching nothing), said,

44

"Fishing"—and I believe meant it, as he was one of the most straightforward people I have ever known. When, at the age of fourteen, I asked him if he thought he'd hit any enemy soldiers with artillery fire during the Second World War, he thought for a few seconds and said solemnly, "I hope so."

It wasn't the answer anyone might have expected from the peace-loving son of a clan of New England Quakers. And not until many years later could I appreciate that it wasn't jingoism that had prompted his response but his refusal to shelter in any sort of personal revisionism. He had gone overseas to do a job, had done that job, and was not about to invalidate his commitment by claiming he hadn't meant any harm.

On another occasion, in my presence, a Toronto car salesman told him the price of a new vehicle, and my dad pulled out his checkbook and pen. The dealer said, "Hume, that's only the starting price—you can bargain," upon which my dad blurted, "I don't want to bargain! If that's not the price, tell me what the price is!"

It drove my mother nuts that when my dad quit a job, as he did seven times during his long years in education, he felt morally obliged to quit before he sought new work.

More pertinent to the subject at hand, he was chief duffer and incompetent among family anglers, an all but comic-strip counterpoint to everything everybody else seemed to know and believe about fishing—everything that, as a kid, I myself wanted to know and believe about catching fish and about the heroic men who caught them. Who *were* these guys, with their talk of fly-tying and migrations and thermoclines; their complicated rods and reels; their coffee tables and outhouses stacked with magazines that spoke of Great Northerns and World Record Muskies, of Lusty Lakers that could battle you for an hour or more and sometimes win?

Perhaps because such magazines represented everything about fishing that was foreign to us, I was fascinated by them—or at least by their covers, which invariably depicted a chuff-looking mesomorph balanced precariously in the back of a smallish motorboat, teeth glistening, rod bent double as his quarry, a five- (or perhaps 105-) pound largemouth, leapt from the water with a Vegas-worthy lure in its jaws.

In seditious fantasy, I see my dad on the cover of *Angler* or *Argosy*—his inflexible rod, his creaky reel, his rotten net, his can of worms, his old khaki pants belted a little too high. A speech bubble emerging from his mouth encompasses an apt quote from Shakespeare or Keats or the Bible, his great loves.

The magazine fishermen had either movie-star hair or battered but rakish fedoras, perhaps with a trout fly attached. And they caught fish—caught big ones! There they were, catching them, right on the covers of glossy magazines!

Adding to my fascination, there was often a boy in the boat, a freckled kid in a plaid shirt who clearly caught his own share of whoppers and was ever so proud of his dad for his capabilities in the fish-slaughtering stakes.

The advertisements inside were for Export A and Seagram's Crown Royal and Old Kentucky Bourbon—commodities that all true fishermen consumed as they exchanged off-color jokes back at the lodge after an invigorating day on the water.

My dad, by comparison, didn't smoke or drink or swear. We didn't even own a motorboat—fished out of an old wooden punt built by my grandfather in the dark ages before my birth and as leaky as an orange crate. And whereas every successful angler we knew had a compartmentalized tackle box full of lures and gizmos for every circumstance and species, we had a tackle "heap," a rueful muddle of busted rods, seized reels, and knotted line that occupied a chipmunk-infested corner of the cabin boathouse. The pip of our gear was a tangled spool of monofilament that someone had bought years earlier from Rocket Richard and that bore a microscopic likeness of his signature. Through most of my childhood I used a rod that didn't even have a reel; the green cotton line was simply wound around the pole, which you turned in your hands to let your hook down. Our neighbor Mr. Workman, who drove a three-ton Buick Four-Holer about twice the heft of our lumpish Dodge Crusader, had muskie lures in his tackle box that were bigger than any fish I'd ever caught. We jigged, he trolled, although he could also cast a Hula Popper 150 feet out into the lake.

My uncle Hal, a fundamentalist preacher, disdained worms (our bait of choice) in favor of frogs and crayfish. He had two casting rods and a store-bought shillelagh for conking the big ones when they made too much fuss in the bottom of the boat. He also had a factory-manufactured anchor, a hinged marine item, while the Wilkinses' anchors varied from paint cans filled with pebbles to cinder blocks to plain old stones that invariably slipped their knots, releasing us to the wind just at the point when the giant bass was about to leap from the water with our hook in its cheek and our half rubber worm dancing on its lips.

Our teetering boathouse held not so much boats as what was left of boats that should long ago have been taken to the township dump, or broken up and burned.

At least in memory, we began every fishing endeavor by cursing this memorable fiasco and trying to "sort something out." We ended each adventure by firing whatever we'd sorted back onto the heap.

I have detailed memories of the only fishing trip I ever took with my dad—a day jaunt by canoe to Gullwing and Echo lakes, a few miles from our cabin. That I hardly slept the night before and was up at seven a.m. assembling paddles and gear was indicative, surely, of my abiding desire to go on a "real" fishing trip—and perhaps equally of my sublimated desire to spend time with my dad. Predictably, by late morning the trip had degenerated to the level of all our other fishing outings. Naturally, we had not caught anything, in large part because we were endlessly snagged on weeds and rocks and whatever other detritus conspired to grab our hooks. At one point my dad snagged the stem band of the canoe, which by noon hour was leaking to the point where we were spending more time bailing than fishing. We had a frying pan. However, at shore lunch, with no fish to fry (and having eaten our four wieners in the canoe), we resorted to our emergency can of beans, discovering only as we gathered sticks for a fire that we had forgotten the matches and would have to eat the beans cold.

We didn't *always* get shut out—at least I didn't. Once, as a nine-year-old, I caught a six-pound carp, an iridescent tribute to the wonders of evolution, in the shallows of the St. Lawrence River, near Cornwall, Ontario, where we lived. I experienced a fierce sense of accomplishment and satisfaction as I handed it to my mother an hour later, and throughout the afternoon imagined it front and center on the dining table, tricked out with lemon and parsley and an array of side dishes fit for the feast that I had so honorably and heroically provided. I was understandably dismayed when a half hour before dinner my mother announced gently that she'd bought something else for the meal, something that wouldn't keep, and that the fish would have to wait. I was further dismayed when, in the morning, she broke the news that my prize quarry had begun to "turn" and that at some point after I'd gone to bed my dad had taken it out and buried it at the back of the garden, where it would function at least as compost for the beans and squash and potatoes that, in a fairer world, would have been its sidekicks on the table.

A year or so later, my uncle Everett, an occasional visitor to our summer cabin, gave us a carton of old gear: casting rods and downriggers, as well as a battery-powered fish locator, one with a little black screen, on which it was claimed you could see fish beneath your boat. Predictably, we couldn't figure the thing out—fortunately, didn't need it, in that we had our own method for locating fish, namely, looking deep into the aptly named Clear Lake, where you could see bottom, and sometimes fish, in twenty-five feet of water. For me, at the time, that was a large part of the joy of it all—watching them come along. It never even occurred to me as a kid that you could catch a fish in turbid water. How could you see it? How could it see the bait? I have always been intensely visual, my obsession such that as a preschooler I famously asked my mother if you could still see after you were dead. If not, being dead was probably even worse than I had suspected.

On account of these psycho-visual fixations, I was all the more impressed many years later when my friend Steve Lawson, who lives in exquisite harmony with the rain forest and sea on Wickaninish Island, a few miles off Tofino, British Columbia, explained to me in a taped interview that as a young man he had been able to *smell* fish deep beneath the surface of the Pacific, and identify them by species, even as he passed in a Zodiac at twenty-five miles an hour. He said, "I could differentiate between herring, anchovies, coho, anything. I'd just stop the boat, throw out a lure, and we'd catch the species I'd smelled. Commercial fishermen used to look at me as if I were a madman, or just a liar. Then years later, a couple of them came up to me and said, 'You know what you used to tell us about smelling the fish? Well, you're right. It's the fishes' essential oils floating to the surface. The more agitated they are in their feeding, the more of it rises, and the better you can detect them.'"

One of our problems, Steve surmised, "is we've stopped trusting our senses—don't believe what they have to tell us until we see it corroborated in print or on television. The senses are like muscles: you either use them or lose them. And once they're lost, so much else is lost, too, in the way we know and understand the world."

Well said—and well exemplified for me three or four years later on a two-day fishing trip to Lac des Mille Lacs, near Ignace, in northwestern Ontario. By mid-afternoon of our first day out, our little party had a couple of pike, half a dozen walleye, and a whitefish on the stringer. Our cooler was empty, and the sun had burned a dreary white hole in any enthusiasm we might have had for carrying on.

Out of his evolving funk, my friend Eric Stoneman said, "Did you know you can identify fish by their smell?"

"Who can?" I said.

"I can."

Within seconds, Eric's fifteen-year-old son had his hands clamped over his dad's eyes from behind, and I had a three-pound whitefish beneath his nose.

"Whitefish," he said confidently.

I held up a walleye, and he said, "Walleye."

Reluctant to believe that his nose could be that sensitive, I picked up a chunk of rough-cut two-by-eight, a discarded piece of barn flooring that had been used as a fish-cleaning board throughout the summer and was rank with the juices of at least four species. Eric sniffed at it for several seconds at close range but said nothing.

"So, what is it?" I demanded.

"Hemlock," he said quietly. "It's hard to distinguish from spruce."

IF THERE IS a mystery to the Wilkinses' incompetence as fishermen, it is amplified for me by my lifelong awareness that at heart we loved fishing—just never got anywhere with it. Maybe, in some perverse way, that is how we liked it. A few months after my dad died, in 2001, I read in one of his journals that he had "always wanted to be a better man . . . but not enough actually to be one." Likewise, we may have *wanted* to be better fishermen but not enough actually to *be* better.

On the scale of issues that have measurably diminished my existence over the years, our incompetence as fishermen simply does not register. What does register in a small way as I look back on my boyhood is a sense that, while all sorts of activities might have become a conduit to my dad, fishing, more than some, really could have been one, as it often is between fathers and sons. However, for it to be so, if only indirectly, would have demanded of my dad a greater willingness to communicate, to participate with his kids, to express himself, in particular his love for me and my sisters, which went radically unspoken throughout our years as children and teenagers. His letters to us when we moved away were signed "Sincerely, Dad," or, on occasion, "Affectionately, Dad." It was the best he could do. His mother had died giving birth to him, and the template for nurturing had apparently gone missing in the loss. Indeed, one of the most poignant of our family stories involves the events surrounding my dad's birth the day after the *Titanic* went down in April 1912. On the night of the disaster, my grandmother, Birdie Wilkins, wrote a letter to my great-aunt, in which she expressed a wish that what had been for her an uncertain and agonizing pregnancy could *please* now just be over. Farther down the page she lamented the loss of "all those lives aboard that big ship."

Her own life ended in agony the following morning. I was not told about this until I was ten years old, at which point an aunt read me my grandmother's letter. I was an impressionable kid, and from the moment I heard the words, I equated her death and my dad's birth—and in a sense still do—not just with the loss of "all those lives aboard that big ship" but with more personal and complicated issues, some of which trickled down to me.

Better communication on my dad's part would certainly have mitigated my sense of his sometimes striking ineptitude. I had no idea, for example, that he had been not just a soldier, as he liked to depict himself—a sort of feckless Beetle Bailey—but a highly capable war hero, a guy twice mentioned in dispatches for bravery in the line of fire, as noted in documents hand-signed by King George VI and still in the family's possession.

At my dad's funeral one of his war buddies told me (as he himself never had) that during the Italian, French, and Belgian campaigns, my dad's job with the Royal Canadian Dragoons, a Montreal artillery unit, was to get in behind enemy lines, incognito, and to establish radio communications with the men back in the trenches. It was a job for which he volunteered—and one of the most dangerous known to ground warfare, in that its practitioners were ruthlessly punished, or simply executed, by the Germans if they were caught. One of my favorite stories about my dad is that late in the war, as the Canadian artillery swept up through Italy on mop-up, my dad, working in plain clothes three or four miles behind the retreating German lines, took the opportunity to go into Rome, where he had his picture taken by an Italian street photographer on the Spanish Steps outside the apartment where John Keats, his favorite poet, had died of tuberculosis a century earlier. The photo is my most treasured memento of him—one that I emulated in 2008, when I myself visited Keats's apartment, which is now a kind of museum to the English poet.

How could we have known such things—things surely at the heart of who he was—when he never spoke of them, even though it had all happened just a few years prior?

At times I suspect I have been as guilty as my dad of lousy communication with my children. Not that I have any great mischief or heroism to report. But there *are* stories to tell, a sense of what it has meant to be afoot on the planet, of what I have stood for, of how much I love them. One of my own problems, as I understand it, is that I have put the bulk and best of what I know, what I have to tell anybody, into the writing of a dozen or more books, some of them very personal—have spent years sitting in a room by myself. And have perhaps accepted too readily that it was enough, that I've said what I have to say. *If you're interested, you can look it up* sort of thing.

I am increasingly aware of this shortcoming as I cruise into my sixties, in effect running out of time. Which is why when, in June of 2013, my son Matt, with whom I had not fished in years, phoned me from a thousand miles away suggesting we go on a little fishing trip, I was quick, was in fact eager, to agree. Among other things, it would be a chance to talk, to bridge what I had begun to recognize as a new generation of silences.

At age twenty-five, Matt has his own war stories—largely untold, at least to me. On the day he turned sixteen, for example, he was involved in a horrific car accident, saw his closest friend, another Matt, from whom he was inseparable, fatally injured in the seat beside him. Even though he was not driving, he endured days under the impression that he was to blame for his friend's death. He said nothing. Grew surly. Quit school. Went to work in a restaurant. Learned the trade. Still said nothing. Would not participate in any sort of psycho- or emotional therapy. Rebelled at even the hint of any question as to how he felt about it all, what was going on inside. On the one occasion he agreed to talk to a psychologist, who was willing to meet him at a doughnut shop, he walked out on him, declaring that he wasn't interested in talking "to a guy in a green golf shirt."

His silence on the matter has lasted nine years and persists today, although he is at least now happy to talk about other things—loves art, likes books, enjoys ideas. Speaks occasionally about himself.

Even as a five-year-old, Matt was somebody I could fish with—and did, on Clear Lake, where he once said he wanted to catch a "smoked salmon" like the ones his uncle Jim brought to the cabin. He had a knack, and several times caught quite decent bass, which in paper silhouette got applied to the Trophy Wall.

Eventually his interest waned. By thirteen or fourteen, he was into other things—dirt bikes and board sports, and by fifteen, activities to which I no longer had access.

On the day after we agreed to go, he phoned again, imploring me to go out and buy some decent tackle, some new rods, some lures, some line, a net, a tackle box. All of which I heartily agreed to.

He said, "It'll make all the difference."

Key to the new gear was a pair of Pflueger rods and reels, which on the day Matt arrived were yet to be wound with line, an apparently easy job that in the end provoked an hour or more of frustrated debate, then quarreling, as we fussed with the uncooperative monofilament, attempting to get the kinks and loops out, agonizing over which direction, clockwise or counterclockwise, it might best be wound onto the reels . . . *no, the other way . . . no, the OTHER way . . . turn the thing over . . . pull on it . . . you have to keep it tight . . . why don't you just leave me alone with it, Dad . . . I can do it if you'd just get outta here!*

The next morning, line wound, tackle boxed, food and tent stowed, we set off by canoe, zigzagging a dozen hard miles up Nine Mile Lake into a brisk north wind. In the moments before we launched, Matt told me confidently that he wanted to be in the stern, in control. He took pleasure in outpaddling me, urging me at times to up my stroke a little, pull a little more water. Otherwise, we didn't say much during more than two hours of paddling, except for occasional muttering over which island, which shoreline, would afford us the best protection from the wind.

At the extreme north end of the lake, as deep in the wilderness as we or anyone will ever have to be, we erected our tent under a couple of giant pines and built a fire pit perhaps a hundred feet away. We hung our food tubs in the trees where bears wouldn't get them and, at perhaps one p.m., slipped the canoe back into the lake and for the next seven hours moved from bay to bay, pool to pool, weed bed to weed bed, doing what we had come to do. When we talked, it was about bait choices and wind, and which shallows and weeds might provide the best possibilities, or any possibilities at all. For a while, we beached the canoe and fished from shore, clambering over three-billion-year-old granite, trying various lures and spinners, casting like the amateurs we were, unsnagging or cutting line as necessary. On a couple of occasions, we sent rubber worms, purple ones, flying across the water.

We did not quit until we had half a dozen keepers—three largemouths, three smallmouths—perhaps forty minutes before dusk. We watched a sunset the color of lilacs and made dinner in the dark, arguing pretty much nonstop over how much oil should be in the frying pan, whether the pan had gotten too hot above the coals, whether the potatoes should be boiled or baked, eventually about whose fault it was that we were having to do everything in the dark, at the risk of tumbling down the granite into the lake.

We ate under a cascade of stars, pausing to look for Orion then returning to our fish, pulling them apart with our fingers, stuffing them in, spitting out the bones in the firelight, arguing again by this time over whether the dishes should be washed before we went to bed. The supposition was that if they were not, they would attract bears. Neatness, Matt reminded me (as I had reminded him a day earlier), is the art of the unimaginative—who, we reminded one another, are seldom eaten by bears. In the end we left the dishes dirty, and stumbled through the trees to the tent, and pissed by the door, and crawled in. And talked about the pleasures of sleeping in the woods. And slept like guys who had paddled all morning and fished for seven hours in the sun.

IT HAS OCCURRED to me during the months since that I know as little about the real lives of my kids as I ever knew about my dad. What thoughts I have on Matt's accident and its aftermath remind me that my dad, too, received no psychological counseling, no therapy or advice, when he came back from the war. If I had not had the advantage of several days at his bedside as he lay dying in 2001, I would never have known, for example, that during the year after his return from overseas, the first of three years spent studying English at the University of Toronto, he lived with explosions of inner turmoil during which he couldn't think, couldn't reason, at times could barely speak. Every night, he walked three or four miles from the university to the apartment that he and my mother and sisters inhabited in Toronto's east end, on some nights stopping on the Bloor Street Viaduct and staring, sometimes for half an hour, into the Don River 150 feet below. There were nights, he told me, when the disorder in his skull got so unruly that it was all he could do to restrain himself from climbing onto the balustrade and jumping off— nights when he prevented himself from doing so "by praying myself another step, and another," until he reached Broadview Avenue, from where he walked up to Withrow to the love of his wife and kids.

AS MATT AND I ate breakfast on the second day of our fishing venture, a $25,000 bass boat roared into our bay, and a man in camo pants took four or five casts and hollered to us that there was nothing in the "gawdam lake" worth catching. And roared off.

I have sometimes wondered whether the Wilkinses, with our trifling catches and amateurish methods, bear some ancient ichthyological curse. At other times I have wondered whether it is perhaps the guys with the bass boats and computerized fish finders who are cursed. I once went fishing with such a guy, and he spent most of the morning fiddling anxiously with his fish finder. When he wasn't doing that, he was racing across the west basin of Lake Erie to where he hoped the non-action would be a little less non.

On the way home, with the canoe atop the car, Matt and I stopped and picked blackberries, which for Matt, who works as a chef, completed a kind of cycle of hunting and gathering, fishing and foraging. "I love this," he told me, although he had not loved the bass we had caught and cooked, finding the largemouths to be "fishy" and thereby somewhat unappetizing. That morning, I had taken two casts and had snagged two of them, which I cooked up for breakfast, while Matt ate fried eggs and hotdogs.

At the cabin, I wondered aloud if he wanted to put cutouts of any of his fish on the wall. He had caught a couple that measured thirteen or fourteen inches. "No," he laughed, and threw his arm around my shoulder and drew me into a hug.

Later, as we fished from the dock, I told him a bit about his grandfather, mentioning that once when I'd asked him what he thought about while he was fishing, he had said, "Fishing."

Matt contemplated this for a few seconds and said, "I think about pretty much everything *but* fishing."

I took a flyer, asked him if he spent much time thinking about his teenage years—say, about his accident and how it had affected him.

"Whadda *you* think about?" he responded without skipping a beat.

"Sometimes about you," I said, adding that mostly I thought about stuff that was too difficult to explain.

It wasn't much of an answer, but it was the beginning of one, perhaps for both of us, and for the moment it was about as close to the truth as I was likely or able to get.

The Grouch of Great Bear

IAN PEARSON

THE MOVIE GAVE men ideas. The movie fueled dreams of misty rivers and sinuous casts and tiny sheaths of metal embroidered with deer hair embedded in the mouths of large trout. The movie made hundreds of thousands of male hearts beat faster and sent Jeep Orvises skidding into over-flowing gravel parking lots beside rivers. The movie looped rocket-tapered lines miscast by high-module graphite rods around the necks of stockbrokers and investment bankers. And the movie got me on the first 737 heading north to Great Bear Lake.

As a fly fisherman, I liked the movie. *A River Runs through It* brought tears to my eyes both times I saw it. The movie reviewer within me (that mystical heart that beats inside all males) detected sentimental direction and a formula script. The fly fisherman within me almost came in my pants. I was nearly thrown out of the film's premiere showing at the Toronto International Film Festival for making guttural noises. A large bug had just planted itself on the side of Brad Pitt's neck. "Uh-oh," cautioned the woman beside me.

"That's not 'uh-oh,'" I protested in a voice that curled ponytails in front of me. "That's a salmon fly. That's the biggest of the western hatches. It only lasts a day or two. All the big fish come up for salmon flies." Sure enough, Brad Pitt threw on a Bunyan Bug and landed a trout the size of Juliette Lewis. "I'm sorry," my neighbor said sheepishly, looking for a vacant seat.

What I didn't like was the aftermath of the movie. Four million people saw A River Runs through It in the early 1990s, and every one of them headed to my favorite rivers. The summer after the movie was released, I arrived at my secret pool on Montana's Madison River to find a dozen anglers had beat me to it. A week later, I found the glorious blue-ribbon trout stretch of the Bow River downstream from Calgary so packed with boats that it looked like a parking lot. One of fly-fishing's great virtues is that it leads me to a realm of solitude and quiet. Now an army of neophyte fly fishermen was running through it. Every time I rounded a bend to find intruders, I would say "fuck off" to an audience of willows and boulders and tumbling water. They proffered no sympathy. Robert Redford had turned me into a massive grouch.

I needed to escape from the crowds, and my salvation came from an unlikely avatar of the natural world—a publicist. Out of the blue, she phoned me to ask if I wanted to join a midsummer fishing junket to a lodge on Great Bear Lake.

A free week of wilderness fishing. I said yes faster than a cut-throat slamming a stone fly.

Great Bear Lake, in the Northwest Territories, is one of the best untouched fishing Edens in the world. The world's eighth-largest lake has never been commercially fished, and only about four hundred fishermen travel to its icy waters every year. It is full of fish, famous for its enormous lake trout (a 72-pounder was caught in 1996) and the plentiful arctic grayling in nearby rivers. Plummer's Arctic Lodges run the only three lodges on the 12,000-square-mile lake. Formerly the domain of meat fishermen who basked in the bloody glory of piles of twenty- and thirty-pound lake trout, the lodge now enforces a catch-and-release policy to protect the ancient and fragile fish population of Great Bear Lake. (Because the water is so cold and the growing season so short, a forty-pound lake trout may be forty to sixty years old.)

Plummer's also offers arctic char fishing at its Nunavut outpost on the Tree River near its mouth to the Arctic Ocean. The triple delight of pursuing lake trout, grayling, and arctic char in a single week promised an intermediate fly fisher-man like myself the dream of a lifetime. There would be few other fishermen to jostle with. There would be dozens of fish looking at every cast I threw. Only the small matter of ability stood between me and a fishing epiphany.

A 5,600-FOOT GRAVEL runway brings a chartered 737 almost to the doorway of Plummer's main lodge, which is tucked just above the Arctic Circle on the northern arm of

Great Bear Lake. But in a sense, you never land. For the first few days I had a sensation of floating. First, there was the striking image of the jet's shadow over the tundra, a symmetrical human beacon on a formless land. On my first venture on the lake, the pellucid waters of Great Bear Lake allowed the light to create a shadow of the boat on the lake bottom when it was fifteen or twenty feet deep. Above, no borderline split the blue of the cloudless sky and the reflective placid skin of the massive inland sea. In the water, cruising lake trout would cast their own shadows, doubling their numbers to human eyes. I felt part of their liquid world.

The fish, unfortunately, weren't particularly interested in connecting with me. My guide, Doug, had taken me to the ruggedly beautiful Narakay Islands, which looked like rusty chunks of the Scottish Highlands plopped indiscriminately into the vast blue plain of the lake. Lake trout patrolled the shelf around the islands in search of any minnows or bugs to help fatten them up for the long winter ahead. I cast a Woolly Bugger into their feeding lane. It's a long, black underwater fly fashioned from marabou feathers. In the water, it imitates a leech, although I hadn't checked whether there were any leeches in Great Bear Lake.

The first trout I cast to ignored this exotic intruder. The second did the same. I couldn't get the line deep enough for the third and fourth fish to even notice the fly. I realized that the downside of fishing in pure wilderness is that the fish were going to be wild as well. The best fancy-pants marabou wasn't going to impress them one bit.

I sat in the boat trying to calculate the number of minutes of the day when I was in a bad mood. Possibly all the time when I wasn't fishing, and probably most of the time when I was—if I wasn't catching fish. I hadn't crossed the Arctic Circle to simply *look* at fish. I asked Doug the guide for advice.

"The water's so clear, the fish are deeper than they look," he said, drinking from a mug of water taken straight from the lake. "You're not getting your fly deep enough. Let's troll."

Troll! Suggesting trolling to a fly fisherman is like putting a paint-by-numbers set in front of a watercolorist. Most of the art in fly-fishing is in the casting: dragging your line from the back of a boat isn't fly-fishing, it's heresy.

So I did it. I put a silver streamer on the end of my leader, added a piece of split shot, and let the line sink. Doug started the motor, and we trolled the minnow-like fly along the shelf. Within half an hour, we had caught and released six lake trout. It wasn't fly-fishing, but it was catching fish. I was in an extremely good mood.

THE MOOD LASTED until dinner, when I was sequestered at a table with the publicist and the only other journalist on the junket, an Englishman who had no interest in fishing or, apparently, anything else. When a plate of succulent arctic char arrived, he declared, "Wouldn't it be great to have a Big Mac right now?" I couldn't connect with anything he said. Across the dining room, the paying fishermen were roaring at each other's stories, but I wasn't allowed to speak with them. (Which was fair enough: someone who popped four grand on a trip didn't need a stranger asking them questions.)

To make matters worse, the Englishman was to be my fishing companion for the week. He was a hopeless fisherman, tangling his trolling gear every ten minutes, complaining about the monstrous difficulty of putting a rod over the back and letting out line, and nattering all the time about how boring fishing was and what a bad sleep he had had because of the long days and how nothing happens up here. I started concocting a fly-fishing murder mystery in my head. If you murdered someone on Great Bear Lake—say, an English flibbertigibbet—how could you get away with it? How would you dispose of a body? If you did it at Tree River on the Arctic Ocean, decaying human flesh could be mistaken for a narwhal carcass ...

MY FORTUNES TURNED when the lodge's manager realized I wasn't getting the casting opportunities I wanted. "Tomorrow we'll get you some real fly-fishing," promised Chummy Plummer over a steak dinner. "Dad will take you up to a grayling river that hasn't been fished in two years."

Warren Plummer was a pilot who got the northern fishing bug when he first flew up to Great Slave Lake in 1938. He built his first fishing lodge there in 1949 and established the main Great Bear lodge in 1969, dragging the buildings 150 miles over the ice in winter. He took over the other two camps when his competitors went out of business. While his son

Chummy ran the camps, Warren kept a paternal eye on the camp's aircraft—an Otter, a Cessna, and a fifty-year-old DC-3.

The Otter took us an hour north of the lodge, beyond the tree line and over defeated old mountains lined with wrinkles of green lichen. We landed on a lake that Warren refused to identify so he could make sure it would be another two years before the next person dangled a line in the water. The aircraft parked near the outlet of the lake, where a small river meandered through banks lined with stunted willows. "There." Warren pointed to the river. "Anywhere on the edge of the current, you'll catch grayling."

God invented arctic grayling to soothe the egos of fly fishermen. It is a lovely fish, with a slender purple-gray body and an immense fanlike fin coming out of its back. Because it is farsighted and a voracious insect-eater, it will hit almost any dry fly you float on the surface. Its scientific name is *Thymallus arcticus,* for the thyme-like smell it gives off when first leaving the water. The dorsal fin has amatory uses, as somewhat breathlessly noted by W. B. Scott and E. J. Crossman in *Freshwater Fishes of Canada:* "During spawning, the male curves the extended dorsal fin over the female almost like a clasping organ, the female gapes, there is vigorous vibration, the male gapes, sex products are discharged and somewhat covered by the material stirred during vibration."

The French name for grayling is *ombre arctique,* which is apt, because grayling are completely camouflaged in the water. I have never seen a grayling in a river except on the end of my line. On my first cast on this mystery river halfway between Great Bear Lake and the Arctic Ocean, a fine eighteen-inch-long grayling hit my imitation caddis fly the second the fly hit the water. For the rest of the morning, I caught a grayling on almost every cast and on every fly I tried.

Grayling's strength compensates for their gullibility, for they fight with the ferocity of a salmon. By lunchtime I had caught and released about forty fish, and killed one for the fish-chowder shore lunch. After lunch I landed maybe another thirty, including a four-pound beauty that rocketed from a deep pool to hammer my imitation grasshopper, ignoring the fact that the nearest real grasshopper was probably a thousand miles south.

In terms of numbers, it was the most successful day of fishing of my life. But I wanted a quarry that would test me. I was ready for arctic char.

THE TREE RIVER, the site of Plummer's outpost camp for arctic char, is a whitewater torrent that rages through a bed of boulders on its way to the Arctic Ocean. The current is punctuated by calm pools and stretches of flat water, which hold arctic char as they rest on their journey upstream to spawn. Looking at the surging white water, it was easy to see why the crimson-hued char is considered one of the strongest sport fishes in the world. "If the fish can swim up those rapids," you think, "what will it do to a fly line?"

I found out shortly after arriving at Tree River on the DC-3. The other fishermen were spin-casting, and had staked out the calm pools. I gazed into a riffle close to the bank and saw something that looked like a red log except that it moved slightly forward and then backwards. Three or four other logs were treading against the current in the same manner. They were giant arctic char.

I put a weighted stone-fly nymph on my leader and cast it upstream. The current eased it in front of the nose of a char. Wham! A scarlet torpedo tore out thirty yards of line before jumping straight up in the water. I felt a fear I'd had only once before in my life—in a car crash. It was the doomed resignation that I had got myself into something terrifyingly powerful that I couldn't control. The fish weighed perhaps twenty pounds and was by far the biggest fish I had ever hooked on a fly line.

The char tore out my line at will and swam downstream into the rapids. All I could do was to clamber and slip over the wet boulders while trying to keep some line on my reel. The fish was trolling me, making me pay penance for my follies with lake trout and grayling. It held steady in the white water, and I was able to reel in more line and keep the line taut.

Once again it leapt, proving why red is the color of anger. When it raced again, I ran with it for another forty yards alongside the rapids. There, I tried to turn the fish's head to guide it into a patch of calm water. The fish snapped its head the other way and bolted into the heaviest part of the rapid. I tried to keep my line taut, but when I reeled in, the fish was gone.

I hooked three smaller char in that riffle, and each made a similar escape in the fast water. Finally, a thunderstorm sent me packing back to the camp in time for dinner. The clouds lifted around eleven p.m., and a couple of hours later, the midnight sun finally dipped slightly below the horizon. The river soaked up the crimson of the sky and snaked through the valley like a giant triumphant char.

It was the color of *my* char, the 20-pounder that would have been the crowning achievement of my fishing career. But losing that fish probably taught me more than if I landed it. Fly-fishing wasn't about solitude, and it wasn't about the right or wrong way to catch fish. It wasn't even about catching fish, whether none at all or way too many. Fly-fishing was all about connecting, however briefly, with something larger than yourself. And for a moment, I wasn't feeling grouchy at all.

Fishing 'round My Father

KENNETH KIDD

THE LURES ARE all still there—the Mepps #5, the Spin Hula Dancer, the two-inch Rapala, the Jitterbug, the rubber crayfish, and a personal favorite, the Heddon Dying Flutter, with the price, $1.65, permanently inked onto its underbelly.

Nearly all of them I'd bought as a small boy, saving my weekly allowance and collecting discarded pop bottles in the ravines that surrounded our east Toronto neighborhood like veins, bottles that brought pennies' worth of riches when returned for their deposits.

Whenever I felt sufficiently flush, I'd troop through the factory district on the other side of one ravine to the sporting goods section of Canadian Tire, carefully avoiding the Peek Freans bakery, from whose trucks we kids used to steal cookies. None of the lures ever worked, unless you started with the weird conceit that their chief purpose was ensnaring weeds or getting caught on Precambrian rock under the water out front of the family cottage in the Kawarthas.

For decades, those lures have sat in the same tackle box, just inside the door of the log cabin that my father built almost single-handedly. I can still picture him carrying huge logs on his slim shoulders, relying mostly on his massive hands for stability, as if acting out some primal Scottish need to build in a new land—with cabers, if possible—just as generations of Scots had done before him. As if in punctuation, the cabin door even has a keyed iron lock of truly medieval proportions, an immigrant, like my father, from the land of oatmeal and whisky.

I have scant memories of ever fishing with my father, fishing being just another one of those things we didn't do together. He had a cabin to build, and later a three-bedroom cottage farther from the lake, where the land rises steeply. There would have been the odd venture with him across the bay, to where a river flows into the lake and the fishing was reputedly good, possibly even home to the six-foot muskellunge said to be lurking somewhere, the fish one neighboring boy's father insisted was so large it had to be caught and milked once a year. Like most tall tales told by adults, this was never fully explained, much less questioned. But still, it would get any small boy's imagination going.

That particular muskie, of course, never rose to one of my lures. They were so much wasted allowance and pop-bottle money. If you wanted to catch fish, in my case mostly sunfish or yellow perch, worms were the way to go, whether store-bought, if you felt rich, or dug up in a Toronto garden for transport north. But the dirty secret about worms is that the supply on any one occasion never seems to be enough, no matter how much you try to stretch things by cutting each critter into many morsels. So there I was, eight going on nine, nine going on ten, or in some other short-panted season of life, sitting at the end of the dock, bereft of worms. Legs over the side, there was nothing to do but swish a bare hook and lead sinker back and forth through the water, which must have seemed a delectable imitation of something, since that's when the muskie struck.

"Dad! Dad!!!"

It was the biggest fish I'd ever caught, albeit technically hauled in by my father. If he'd been a fishing dad, like others on the lake, he would have known right away that it was an inch and a half short of regulation, but he wasn't, so it fell to the local taxidermist to impart the bad news. An uncle back in the city ended up eating my muskie, since cooking it *chez nous* would have been an insurmountable challenge for my mother, whose kitchen abilities always ran—and I'll say this politely—to the minimalist end of the spectrum.

As I write this now, sitting on the big cottage deck that my octogenarian father recently rebuilt solo (as always), there's a small boy out on the lake, fishing with what must be his father.

I don't really have similar memories. As a wee lad, fishing was mostly a solitary affair by default, given all the property's construction challenges, against which I was then too small and too unskilled to offer much in the way of assistance, though I would soon enough build my own little roofless log cabin, perhaps four feet by eight. This, too, was a solitary pursuit, as was much else in those days before the lake started truly filling up with cottages, many of them now year-round mansions compared with anything that was there in the 1960s.

Solitary, that is, save whenever my little sister was, as very often, too much underfoot, including the time she was underfoot beneath the tree fort in the woods far behind the cottage. I hadn't built the tree fort, but I'd *found* it. Older kids might have originally built it, or perhaps hunters, since it was really just a kind of platform in the trees. To this I could make small amendments, outfitted as I was with a miniature axe of a heft that might these days be illegal for youngsters to wield. And as any small boy knows, the only way to transport a heavy tool from the height of a tree fort to the ground is to toss it overboard and let nature take its course.

"Heads up."

The small axe bounced off my sister's head, though presumably not by the business end, since the nick was relatively small. But still, there was the blood—seemingly gallons of the stuff, pouring out of her. I climbed down, picked her up, and ran as best I could back to the cottage, nearly a mile off.

A panicked family, even the dog, was quickly loaded into the car for a trip to the hospital in Campbellford—everyone, that is, save me, left alone at the end of the road leading to the cottage. I was eleven years old.

Nothing much was said afterward, or at least nothing I can recall, although at weddings and family gatherings ever since I tend to get introduced—or worse, recognized by my sister's friends, courtesy of prior intelligence—as the attempted murderer in their midst.

Of such things families are defined, I suppose, and ours never seemed much different from the others around us. As much as I now adore and revere my father, I cannot say this was always true, though I'm not sure how much this stemmed from our own faults and failings and how much from the general milieu in which we both found ourselves. Growing up, I don't recall any boy being close, truly close, to his father. It just didn't seem the normal course. Fathers then were a kind of Doric pillar, always working long hours, doing chores, issuing commands from on high; and if they decided to go off and do something recreational as their reward, *sans famille*, then that was the way of the world. Or at least the old world, the one that even then was starting to seem anachronistic amid the U.S. civil rights movement, the riots in Detroit, Vietnam, hippies, and the general mistrust of anyone over thirty—grown-ups, or "grups," as they were called in one episode of *Star Trek*.

Nor was my father much versed in any kind of child-rearing, having been an only child in a place like Scotland, the Depression-era deprivations of which would not have ameliorated a culture whose treatment of kids tends to vacillate, at the best of times, between giving them sweets and giving them a clout in the lug.

Neither of us was in a position to choose who we were. I do, however, have an idea of what it might be like to learn fishing from one's father, especially fly casting, since a variant of that teaching relationship has marked my entire life.

Like most of his peers, my father left school in Wishaw, Scotland, when he was fourteen; he worked briefly in steel and cement factories before becoming an apprentice plasterer. It was better than working up at t'mill, but still not the brightest future amid Britain's postwar malaise, so he eventually decamped for a new life in Canada, met the gal, began a family, and started his business.

There are pictures of me in tartan shorts, not much more than a toddler, and if my father wasn't playing jazz on the phonograph then it was bagpipe music, especially a record from what must have been a military tattoo, the voiceover announcing, "Here come the MacGregors."

Dad was bigger than life in those days, not least when we wrestled, which is maybe where the trouble started. I still have acute memories of him pinning me, a tiny child, to the floor. Struggle as I might, I was helpless. Even now, I can feel the anger and frustration of those moments, which is why when my own daughter and I started to play-wrestle, I always made it a theatrical event, complete with me as Monty Pythonesque announcer introducing her ("The Great Bardinio") and me ("Meadow Muffin"), the obvious loser of the match.

Freudians can have their field day, I suppose, but however unwittingly, my father taught me an invaluable lesson that perhaps he had never had the chance to learn on the unforgiving, grimy streets near Glasgow.

So the two of us, my father and I, carried on through my childhood, with not a very great deal in common save familial ties. Fishing certainly wasn't for him, but cycling was—a personal passion he'd imported with himself from Britain.

Cycling was another one of the things we didn't do together, though as a very young boy I was hauled off to country roads to stand in the sun and watch races. These seemed to involve a lot of Italian men with shaved and oiled legs, which just didn't seem manly somehow, especially not next to hockey, the sport I adored, murder and poetry on ice. Hockey never much resonated with Dad. I'd wince whenever he referred to the goalie as the "keeper," as if he were on a British football pitch instead of on the ice, or criticized how a Leafs game was playing out. The old dump-and-chase was a tactic that never made any sense to him, no matter how often you might explain its sometime utility.

My father, of course, couldn't skate, had never played the game, so hockey, too, became one of those things we never did together. There was, for a time, cross-country skiing, until a bout of frostbite pretty much curbed whatever enthusiasm I might have developed for the sport.

What we did come to share—although at first "share" wasn't quite the right word, my position being so clearly subordinate—was construction work. Weekends would find me on Dad's job sites, fetching, cleaning, eventually mixing plaster or perlited gypsum, for 50 cents an hour, then 75, then a dollar.

Until I bolted to work instead for another boy's father, who owned a chromium plating company in the black-hued grimness of Corktown—a part of the city best remembered for its ancient taverns with names like The Derby, their floors covered in sawdust, an incongruous separate entrance for "Ladies and Escorts," and a very liberal interpretation of the province's liquor laws with respect to minors.

For $1.25 an hour, I had the privilege of sweeping leaden dust from floors and gangways, from which you'd climb down into massive iron tanks to slop out the remaining liquid carbon with a bucket. No matter how much you scrubbed after work, it was virtually impossible to get the smell of the factory out of your hair and skin, much less remove all of the carbon blackness seemingly fused to your fingertips.

I can't imagine this much pleased my father, which is perhaps why he kept asking me whether I'd been paid yet. When I admitted the answer was no, Dad duly marched off to demand his son's wages from the other boy's father. I can imagine that scene, Dad on the doorstep with his huge hands, accent now menacingly thick, the ex-boxer, ex–British Army, looking like a belligerent Sean Connery, whom he's always resembled. When my father first arrived in Canada, Italian construction workers would pick fights with him. This was their first mistake. The second was calling him "a skinny Englishman," thus ensuring that the beating was doubly brutal. I got my money, which is little wonder.

And so I drifted back into my father's employ, serving a kind of ad hoc apprenticeship as a plasterer. The genius of that arrangement might not have been apparent to me then, but it is now. By teaching me a trade, Dad was giving me portable skills that would ensure I never went hungry, or that would put me in good stead if I ever decided to take over the business. But his real, unspoken message was this: You really don't want to do this backbreaking work for the rest of your life.

Except that, in a sense, I have—renovating my own homes and investment properties at night and on weekends and holidays since I was in my twenties. Which means that, for nearly my whole life, whenever I've held a hawk and trowel in my hands, and especially when I've used my lathing hammer, the kind that looks like a hatchet, I have felt my father's presence, as if he's somehow inside of me, inside my arm. Our movements are all the same, in sync. Had he been a fly fisherman, and had he shared the sport with me, I'm sure I'd now be feeling the very same sensation with every cast.

I might even be uttering whatever fish-related expressions he would have had, just as I now parrot some of his construction sayings: "We're not building a piano," if the task at hand requires no particular fussiness. Or, "A blind man would be glad to see it," if there is some unforeseen or unavoidable imperfection in the completed work.

As it happens, fishing of any kind pretty much left my life for decades, until a few work colleagues arranged for us all to spend a day on the Grand River in southern Ontario with Ian Colin James, the guide who used to talk about fly-fishing on Peter Gzowski's old radio show, *Morningside*.

Until then, I'd never even held a fly rod, but by a quirk I had come to possess one—an ancient eight-and-a-half-foot Montague Holloglass that had been left behind in the third-floor cedar closet of the house my wife and I bought nearly twenty years ago in Toronto's High Park neighborhood. And so, having picked up a cheap reel—it was a test, after all, this fly-fishing—I found myself in the water with Ian and three friends near Fergus, Ontario, just downstream from what everyone calls the Humpty Dumpty bridge, a wry reference to some guy who reputedly fell off it and came to a bad end.

To say that Ian is a big guy doesn't quite do justice to calves the size of country hams. He has a way of filling a river the way he does a room, with an accent that can't help but draw attention, and of a type I've long known. At first he said he was from Glasgow, the way someone from a little-known town outside Toronto might tell strangers abroad that they're from the city itself, for the sake of geographic simplicity.

It turns out Ian is actually from farther up the Clyde, from Viewpark, a kind of suburb of Motherwell on the road to Hamilton, near my father's hometown of Wishaw. In my dad's time, Motherwell was the happening place if you weren't going all the way to Glasgow in search of the better dance halls. It's also where my father served his apprentice-ship, which in those days meant pushing a barrow around town and doing small jobs and repairs, along the same streets that Ian would later know as a kid.

My paternal grandfather used to walk the five miles or so from Wishaw to Motherwell to watch football matches at Fir Park, back in the days of seatless terraces. I have a photograph of him walking the streets as a man, looking very jaunty, and another one taken in 1920—a group shot of workers at the Lanarkshire Steel Co. Ltd. 27-inch mill in Motherwell. My grandfather is the small boy sitting at the front with the other small boys, arms and legs crossed, his hammer and iron tongs in front of him, propped against his shins. Like most of the men around him, he looks anything but jaunty under his newsboy cap. They all appear so grim, almost menacing, which might have been the expected pose in portraits of that era, but you can't help wondering whether they're not just angry with fate, seething over what it's put all around them, what it's done to them.

I only ever met my grandfather once before he died of Huntington's disease, a cruel end for someone who so loved walking along the Clyde and hiking through the moors. I have no direct memory of him, being then but a wee bairn ferried across the pond by proud new parents. But I still have all of the florins and half crowns that family friends and rela-tives gave me as a baby, as was the custom then—coins worth two shillings and two shillings sixpence in the old currency, their heads graced with King George v or George vi.

Nor do I have any memory of the council row house on West Academy Street where my grandparents lived—he a Scot whose ancestors were mostly commercial fishermen from around Inverness, and she a Yorkshire bride who would never work herself.

In the wake of that visit, my Canadian mother always referred to Scotland in general and Wishaw in particular as a kind of third-world place, coarse and tough and covered in soot, a land of rain and glowing slag heaps and gas meters into which you'd have to insert a shilling in the middle of the night if you had any faint hope of getting warm.

It's from that house, and into that world, that my father ventured out as a boy to catch rabbits with a ferret or tend to his pigeons or cycle the countryside. Or he'd climb Tinto Hill, as I would many years later, carrying a small rock to deposit on the ever-growing cairn at the summit.

And it's to that house that he would have returned, bruised and bloodied, after getting caught stealing scrap metal by the yard's owner, who then instructed his own, much older boy to beat my father within an inch of his life. Dad managed to escape all that, the land of hard men and council houses, which is how his own son would instead come to be standing in the middle of Ontario's Grand River, a Montague rod in hand, being taught how to cast by another son of Lanarkshire.

Ian Colin James first learned to fish with a fly rod on the River Clyde, tutored by a nearly seventy-year-old man inevitably named Jimmy, who'd spent his life working in the steel mills. In Ian's telling, Jimmy was a bit of a hard man, ever quick with his fists, but with a reputation for outrageously good fortune when it came to fishing, which is why Ian's da had pressed him into service.

As Ian writes in *Fumbling with a Flyrod*, comments like "Auld Jimmy kin git fish oot a puddle, 'n' the fish dinna even ken thir in there" just seemed to trail after the man. Ian had fished with his own father, jigging with hand lines for cod and mackerel on the Clyde Estuary, or catching perch and pike in local ponds with bread for bait. But fly-fishing was another matter.

So a six-year-old Ian duly found himself on the Clyde, under a graffiti-riddled bridge, surrounded by broken whisky and wine bottles, hoping that under Jimmy's tutelage he'd catch his first Atlantic salmon. Ian still likes to say how if he caught a fish then, he figured he'd immediately graduate to manhood and be called "mister" down the pub, which is a quaint ambition for a boy then still too young even to be allowed inside a Scottish pub.

Not that he was having much luck, and the sun was going down when he finally tied a size 16 Gravel Bed onto his line, where it joined a size 14 Peter Ross for a two-fly cast into the darkened water. Then it happened: there was something else on the line.

"I got a fish! I got a fish!"

Jimmy was soon enough hustling downriver, net in hand, but the fish in question turned out to be no silver-sided salmon but a five-inch grayling, no matter how much Ian might keep asking whether it could still be a salmon after all.

On which point Jimmy was pretty clear: "Is that wee thing big and silver?"

A much older Ian, the one who immigrated to Canada as my own father had done decades earlier, now refers to me as a fellow Scot whenever we fish together, such are all the Lanarkshire connections. And that especially includes fishing at the Coal Tar Classic, something Ian has co-organized for years as a larkish fundraiser for a charity that helps street kids in Hamilton, Ontario, just down the highway from Toronto, much the way Hamilton, Scotland, is just down the road and across the Clyde from Motherwell.

Given the event's name, it won't surprise that the Classic involves putting two dozen fairly accomplished fly fishers on an industrial pier in Hamilton Harbour, not far from where HMCS *Haida* is now moored as a kind of floating museum of tough and dangerous times, having been commissioned as a Tribal-class destroyer in 1943.

In theory, at least, you could catch pike and bass and even salmon in these waters, but only three fish count in this competition: carp and drum, or sheepshead, and paddlefish, which resemble sharks. There's also the unofficial rule that if you pull up Jimmy Hoffa, you automatically win.

To the happy winner goes a trophy topped by a seventeen-pound hunk of Ontario coal, and one year Ian even managed to land a small piece of coal, having hooked into the zebra mussel attached to it. There ought to have been a special prize for that.

Year after year I've sat with the others on that pier, as often as not in the gray, drizzly days of March, looking out across the harbor to the giant steel mills of Algoma and Stelco, their huge, satanic chimneys billowing darkness.

I'm not sure if it's that particular view or all the times Ian and I have joked about Rangers and Celtic (neither of us gets injured that way, if we joke) and how poorly Motherwell FC are faring (again), or whether it's the growing realization that my own father's days are drawing toward their inevitable close, but it's all filled me with one certainty.

Whether as a kind of homage to Dad, or a way to square my Lanarkshire roots with the fly rod I now hold hammerlike in my right hand, I'm going to have to fish the River Clyde some day. And imagine my father with every cast.

What a Place to Wet a Lion

CHARLES GAINES

*A version of this essay was previously published
in* Forbes Life *magazine.*

THE MEMBERS OF some Zambezi River tribes, I had been told the day before, believe that crocodiles are their reincarnated ancestors, and that the shocking percentage of their people who meet their maker every year via crocodile are individuals who were unkind to their parents. I was brought to a disconcerting recollection of these beliefs by Roelof as soon as I stepped out of the boat onto the jungly shore and took my first cast with a big streamer fly into the murky roil of the Zambezi.

"I'd move a good meter away from the bank, if I were you," he said and smiled. "That way you might at least see the croc before he takes you."

Being backed up to thorn trees while trying to remember every insult visited on my long-suffering father during my adolescence did nothing for my backcast, and as I fished my wide-eyed way down the bank, I was struck with a disturbing irony: I was, after all, here largely because of my father ... Could this be a setup?

Who other than he—an insatiable and world-traveled angler—was responsible for my having eccentrically mooned away my youth over outdoor magazines with dreams of the barramundi and black marlin of Australia, the noble mahseer of India, the dorado of northern Argentina, the fearsome tigerfish of Zambezi? Now, having pursued those dreams as immoderately as a crack addict for over forty years, I had only the tigerfish and mahseer left uncaught from my boyhood wish list. Here I was, finally angling for one of them, botching every cast in a cold sweat of Iron Age magical thinking and feeling ripe for reprisal.

Ridiculous, you say; but were there not omens? Like the dead and rotting eight-pound tigerfish Roelof had found floating in the river that now lay where he had placed it on the bank, seeming to grin at me around its preposterous dentures; or the pair of baboons twenty yards off under a thorn tree who watched me like blood-sport fans, cackling and scratching their asses; or the submerged hippos cruising by with their periscope eyes alight with anticipation. And when the growing dark finally put an end to my timorous and fishless casting, it was with relief that I retired to the boat with Roelof, my irrepressibly cheerful young friend Teddy Grennan, and photographer Håkan Stenlund.

Grilled chicken wings and restorative gin and tonics in hand, we watched a giant blood-orange sun set behind a tableau of wading elephants. "What a place to wet a lion," commented Teddy, then broke into his sorely off-key version of "The Lion Sleeps Tonight," which was to score our entire stay in Zambia. The wretched pun and song somehow bucked me up, and as the boat carried us back upriver in the cooling air toward the camp, I had all but come around when an enormous crocodile crashed into the water from the bank not ten yards away.

"Twelve or fifteen feet," said Roelof. "Magnificent creatures. They have no predators, you know. A croc that big would be close to fifty years old."

About the same age as my father when I was making his life a living hell.

ROELOF SCHUTTE AND his pretty wife, Helen, managed Old Mondoro, one of six safari camps in Zambia's 1,580-square-mile Lower Zambezi National Park. The park was opened in 1983 and has since become, through steady and rigorous conservation efforts, one of the top game-viewing parks in Africa, as well as one of the world's premiere destinations for tigerfish angling. The best months for that angling, September and October, are Zambezi's hottest and driest months. At that time the seventy-five miles of the Zambezi River inside the park are both a magnet and a haven for animals, and their density in and around the river is nothing short of staggering. There are over seventy hippos, for example, to every half mile of river. Day and night they wander near and through the camp, along with elephants, baboons, and African buffalo. Over the next five days at Old Mondoro and its sister camp, Sausage Tree, I could have dropped dozens of flies onto the noses of all of those animals, as well as crocodiles and waterbucks, with no cast longer than sixty feet. I might even have hooked some of them with a *backcast*.

It is this myriad of proximate wildlife that gives angling on the lower Zambezi the surreal, Disneyesque coloration that everyone who has ever fished there mentions. It also has the dangerous tendency of making you feel as if you are in a "park" park—a harmless, Americanized sort of place where the thing over there on the trail to your tent is really a kid named Ralph from Iowa City who is working his way through college by wearing a buffalo getup.

"You don't go anywhere after dark without one of the staff accompanying you," Roelof told us after dinner. "During the day you are free to walk around on your own, but keep your eyes open, and if you see an elephant or hippo or buffalo between you and where you are going, come and get some-one. *Don't* walk up to it."

We were sitting around a fire with Roelof and Helen and a nice couple from London, cigars and port putting the finish-ing touches to a splendid feed of Zambezi bream, taken at a table set outside with linen and crystal, and lit, as were the bar and dining pavilion, by kerosene lanterns. Old Mondoro is the smallest of the lodges in the park (it takes a maximum of eight guests) and less elaborate than some, but Teddy, Håkan, and I were finding it perfectly to our tastes. My spirits had lifted considerably, as they generally do with the ministrations of good food and alcohol, and as I listened to the huffing of hippos from the river and other unidentified coughs and sighings coming from the winterthorn jungle surrounding us, it seemed clear that my earlier fearful funk had been the product of a sullen, self-involved Camusian estrangement. All I needed to do to catch fish and enjoy myself in this wonderland of God's creatures, I decided, was to relax and become one with it.

I had a chance to try out that approach as soon as I was led back to my riverside sleeping chalet—a wonderfully comfortable affair, by the way, made of reed, thatch, and canvas with an open-air bathroom—when the flashlight held by the young man accompanying me picked up a hippo standing just five feet off the path. This, I was told, was Norman, a young bull who disliked fighting, was fond of Helen, and was a frequent visitor to the camp. Wearing a becoming wreath of water hyacinth around his considerable neck, Norman contentedly munched thorn-tree pods as I watched him for four or five minutes. Hippos are said to be responsible for killing more people every year than any animal in Africa, but there was clearly no murderous intent here; and since I admired his hyacinth garland (worn perhaps for Helen?) and have always been more of a lover than a fighter myself, I had no trouble at all becoming one with Norman before toddling off to bed.

Håkan, Teddy, and I had a sunrise breakfast at 5:15 the next morning with Roelof, and by then I had already become one with a white frog, a silver lizard, and a garrulous, long-beaked bird in my chalet, and with hundreds of laughing-doves in the trees around the eating pavilion, whose cooings were our breakfast soundtrack. But all that wasn't even an appetizer for the smorgasbord of at-oneness opportunities we encountered over the next three and a half hours on a walking safari with Roelof, an AK-47-armed park warden, and the couple from London.

Roelof's opening safety lecture ("Don't run unless you are told to. If I tell you to get behind a tree or a termite mound, please do it *now*. Don't take pictures of a charging animal.") struck me as a bit obligatory and overblown as we stood listening to it on the riverbank, which this morning seemed nothing less than a Peaceable Kingdom of plover and Egyptian geese, exquisite white-fronted bee-eaters, a troop of chattering monkeys, and a raft of hippos lying submerged in the river like speed bumps with eyes. As we walked, Roelof pointed out various animal tracks, bird nests, and lion-ant hills, and gave us a fifteen-minute treatise on the sociology and architectural intricacies of a ten-foot-tall termite mound, which, though impassioned, left me incompletely connected to those insects.

A sexy, no-nonsense little female warthog was easier. She pranced up very close to our group and stared at us with attitude, her feisty face, curly mane, and pretty haunches reminiscent somehow of Britney Spears. I had no problem feeling at one with her; nor with four old buffalo bulls lying in a grassy opening who had a grumpy, early-morning look of various joints paining them with which I am too familiar; nor with the herds of skittish impalas, the troops of curious baboons, the great white-bibbed fish eagle eyeing the river for breakfast from the top of a tree. As we wandered quietly in single file among the well-spaced thorn trees, through shafts of candied morning light, learning why hyena dung is white and how to tell the shoulder height of an elephant by its tracks, I fancied I could feel myself emerging from my twenty-first-century cocoon of natural estrangement into a fine primordial empathy. "*Yes,*" I would have shouted to the animals but for Roelof's certain disapproval. "I *feel* your alertness, your curiosity, your fears, your appetites ... "

It was with appetite in particular that I found my strongest empathy toward the end of the long walk when we sat on a termite mound and watched a big bull elephant breakfasting, as I was hoping soon to be, gorging himself on thorn-tree pods, grass, and anything else that came to trunk. Either indifferent to or unaware of our presence, he fed up to within thirty feet of us and was moving closer when the warden knocked loudly on the stock of his rifle, interrupting the old chap's meal and sending him off in an understandable huff.

Partially, perhaps, out of a desire to make up for the warden's rudeness, and partially because of my new empathetic expansiveness, I was led shortly after lunch into nearly getting Teddy and myself stomped into mud holes. On our way back to the chalets for a nap we spied three elephants, very close to Teddy's chalet, drinking out of the river. One of them, a young bull, was missing a tusk and was acting chesty with the other two out of an obvious tusk-envy; this, after we had observed it for a while, seemed to me something I might be able to work with. I strolled down closer to them, Teddy following with his video camera going, and then closer. The elephants turned around to look at us.

"Where do you think their comfort zone stops?" asked Teddy, referring to the invisible line of proximity to elephants that Roelof had warned us not to cross without specifying where exactly it was.

"I'd say about here," I allowed, noticing a distinct change of demeanor in One-Tusk. I was on the point of sharing with him how I myself was missing a big toe when he and the other two began trotting uphill toward us, their ears raised. Teddy and I backed up, then turned and ran. With the elephants hot on our heels, we burst into Teddy's chalet only feet ahead of One-Tusk, who waved his trunk and eyed us malignantly, his great wagging ear filling the open door.

"He could, you know, knock this little building down with—" I turned to Teddy, who was grinning and filming with his video camera.

"Could you put your face between the camera and that guy's head?" he asked me. "Your expression is priceless." But I was already around him, heading for the back wall of the chalet, which was open above waist height . . . and filled with the looming bulk of another elephant.

"Quick, the bathroom!" I said and scurried for it, planning to jump its enclosing wall, but there guarding it stood the third beast. Feeling doomed, I turned around. We were surrounded by ten tons of irked elephants in a tiny thatch hut, and Teddy, whose empathy must extend admirably beyond my own, was filming and saying, "Could you just reach your hand out like you're going to pat him?"

I WOULD LOVE to tell you that, properly chastened by One-Tusk and his friends into an attitude of respectful humility before the great natural world, I went on upriver to Sausage Tree Camp after our near Grizzly Man experience and fished as instinctively and productively as a fish eagle, filling up the boat with the tigerfish of my boyhood dreams. Alas, I cannot.

What I can tell you is that the camp itself, for all its remoteness, is a marvel of creature comforts. You sleep on a sumptuous bed in a spacious Bedouin-style tent made of reeds and white canvas, under linen sheets and a down duvet. Power for lights and fans, and for the hot water for your shower, is provided by a silenced generator. Your meals are cheffed by Honore Kabongo, trained in Paris, and taken on a platform hanging dramatically above the river in the shade of a sausage tree. And your every wish—for a fresh towel by the pool? for another of the addictive "Brian's Specials" from the eponymous bartender?—is attended to, almost before it can be uttered, by your own personal tent valet or by the charming young couple who managed the camp.

Moreover, the camp's owners have judiciously kept all the emollients in harmony with the place and experience it offers, avoiding the cloying ultraluxury of some of the $1,000-a-day African "camps." Pampered as you are, Sausage Tree is much more about what you do there than what is done for you. And there is no shortage of things to occupy your time, all centered as they should be on the astounding wildlife of the park. Every day, you may choose among a variety of ways to observe that wildlife: safaris by foot, boat, or vehicle, and a truly stunning four-hour canoe trip down the lovely Chifungulu Channel, during which you paddle carefully around God's own amount of hippos and crocs while trying to take in the clouds of ibis, egrets, Goliath herons, and other birds, the loafing elephants and buffalo, the bounding impalas and waterbucks. My own favorite activities were the nighttime game drives. The most vivid moments of our trip for me were sitting with a pre-dinner gin and tonic in the back of a slow-moving safari vehicle under the leaning equatorial stars, breathing in the ineffably sweet and nostalgic odor of a freshly fallen night by water, and watching nocturnal animals ghost in and out of the torch held by our guide—a spaniel-size honey badger with a smart white stripe down his back who grunted as he walked; two groups of lions, one comprised of three harried-looking females and seven or eight cubs who play-stalked our vehicle...

And then, of course, there is the fishing (an official and guided activity at Sausage Tree, a do-it-yourself one at Old Mondoro). Most of it is done, often quite productively, with heavy spinning rods and hooks baited with chicken hearts.

If you want to sport for the tigers with fly rods, fine, and you can catch them that way, but you are laying yourself open to the vagaries that always attend refined technique. Such as fish who bite at but won't eat a fly.

Believe me, that was the last thing I had expected from *Hydrocynus vittatus*, the striped river dog, who is a relative of the piranha, grows to over thirty pounds in the Zambezi, and is legendary for his ferocious aggressiveness. But Håkan, Teddy, and I found the river dogs to be as coy as debutantes in their eating habits.

With the hardworking Charles as our guide, we spent hour after blistering hour (the temperature reached 120 Fahrenheit while we were there) pounding the banks from a safari boat with all manner of streamers and poppers, drawing frequent and maddening swirls at the flies and short-takes, but precious few eats. Finally, on the second day, Håkan broke through with a fat 9-pounder that jumped and ran impressively and was then photographed and admired for the awesome piece of work it was: a silver chassis with black stripes, an orange and black tail, and a face full of outsized fangs that looked like it was purchased in the Halloween section of Walmart. Then Teddy, a rank long-rod amateur, caught a small one to yet another chorus of "The Lion Sleeps Tonight." Håkan caught a small one and lost a larger one. Teddy caught *another* small one ... And I began to sour.

I like to think I am long past being competitive about fishing, but this seemed unfair. All I wanted was one good fish (perhaps a tad bigger than Håkan's)—to catch it cleanly, hold and study it for a moment, using the expensive Boga-Grip gadget I had bought for lifting toothy fish without losing a finger, and release it unharmed, as a token set free from an old dream. Oh, and to get a photo of it to hang on my wall.

But by the second afternoon at Sausage Tree, that simple wish had begun to seem cruelly unattainable. I had given my rod to Teddy and was sitting in a snit with a beer, watching all the hippos and things on the bank who now seemed nothing more than pain-in-the-ass impediments to catching my fish. Bitterly, I asked Teddy and Håkan if they knew of another place in the world where, while peacefully angling, you could have your boat turned over by a hippo, lose a leg to a croc as you swam for shore, then, once you had made it, be stomped on by an elephant, gored by a buffalo, and have lions eat what was left of you. Plus your fly rod. So much for empathy.

They both looked at me pityingly.

"Why don't you take a few casts?" said Teddy, and handed me my rod. "I'm worn out from catching these things."

I tied on the biggest, ugliest popper I had, grimly took the bow, cast... and hooked my fish! It jumped gloriously (showing itself to be, in fact, a tad bigger than Håkan's), and everything for a few brief moments was right again with the world. But after Charles had Boga-Gripped the fish and pushed his hand up through its gills to remove the fly, it began to gush blood. I took the Boga-Grip from Charles, both to weigh the fish and to hold its less bloody side up over the water for Håkan to take a photo. *Just one photo,* brothers and sisters, of this fish I had wanted to catch for over half a century! And... well, what can I tell you but the truth? The tigerfish gave a mighty thrash and wrenched the Boga-Grip out of my hand before Håkan could raise his camera.

I stood on the stern seat and watched the dying fish, still attached to the Boga-Grip, being carried by it, struggling, toward the bottom—a vision I wouldn't wish on my worst enemy. I wondered if my father had had moments like this far away from home. If he had, I believed I knew what he would have made of them.

Oh well, I thought. There is still the noble mahseer of India.

Old Friends

JAKE MACDONALD

WHEN I FIRST laid eyes on Paul Quarrington, I wasn't impressed.

I saw his photograph in the book review section of Canada's national newspaper the *Globe and Mail*—a stumpy-looking guy in dark horn-rimmed eyeglasses with a cigar in his mouth and a fishing rod in his hand. He had just won a prize for his latest novel, which apparently was a sympathetic portrayal of a stumpy-looking guy who smokes cigars, drinks too much, and behaves badly. I was living in a remote backwoods community in northern Ontario at the time, writing short stories that weren't winning prizes and working as a fishing guide. Downtown Toronto was a thousand miles to the east, but I still managed to keep up with the literary news and I'd heard of Paul Quarrington. But fishing? I didn't know he fished. And in a schoolboyish kind of way it annoyed me. I thought he should be satisfied to win book prizes—he didn't need to hog fishing too.

I had a friend at the time named Chris, a talented quip-artist who edited the local tourism magazine and had spent many summers working as a fishing guide. Chris happened to be a fan of Paul Quarrington's novels, and one day he informed me that Quarrington was coming to Kenora to do a reading. "You should come," Chris said. "You might pick up a few tips."

"Like what?"

"Like how to write prize-winning books."

"I'll pass, thanks."

A few days later, I was puttering in the kitchen of my houseboat when I heard the tread of heavy footsteps coming up the gangplank. I opened the door and beheld two men standing on the front deck. One was Chris. The other was a stumpy-looking guy in dark horn-rimmed glasses with a cigar in his mouth. Chris smiled. "Jake MacDonald, meet Paul Quarrington."

Chris had attended the reading, enjoyed it, and hijacked Quarrington. After a couple of drinks, we loaded my boat and went walleye fishing. Walleye fishing, in my neck of the woods, is a finesse game in which you twitch a rubber-tailed jig along the bottom and wait for the subtle nudge that indicates a nibbling walleye. It's all done by touch and intuition. It's the sort of fishing that Stevie Wonder would probably be very good at. Chris stood in the front of the boat, dabbing his rod at the water like a witching wand. After a moment, he jerked the rod in mock panic as the rod bowed down against the weight of the fish. "Oh jeez, it's a big one! *Get the net!*"

The pecking order of expertise in our boat quickly established itself. Chris always used to beat me by one or two balls on the pool table and would catch one or two more walleye than me when we went fishing. Now, as always, Chris caught more fish than me, but I caught more fish than Paul Quarrington. I was pleased that we'd done our job as hosts and showed Paul Quarrington where he belonged in the pecking order of writers who also fish—last. Paul gracefully accepted his lowly status and seemed to enjoy our little adventure. *Not a bad guy,* I thought to myself. And when he left, he suggested that we fish together again sometime.

I had the habit of going to Toronto two or three times a year, staying in cheap hotels on Yonge Street and spending my days plaguing magazine editors and book publishers. On my next visit to Toronto I called Quarrington, and he acted as my guide. He knew the city like I knew the hundreds of miles of intricate shoreline and covert fishing nooks in Minaki, and we spent many fine evenings cruising the stone canyons of downtown Toronto, looking for a place to get a drink and watch some music. During some of those visits he and I made an effort to go fishing, pursuing the minimal opportunities available in a city of five million people. On one occasion we rented a boat and went casting for nonexistent pike and bass in the back bays of the Toronto Islands, and spent much of our time picking sludge and used sanitary products off our hooks. On another, we drove up north of the city, looking for rivers and creeks rumored to contain fish. One day, a high-end television producer invited Paul on an excursion for rainbow trout in the Caledon Hills, north of Toronto, and Paul in turn invited me. It was a rare opportunity to fish private property stocked with captive trout, and we were keen. Unfortunately, this was a fly-fishing trip, and I was clumsy with a fly rod, as was Paul. But Allan the TV producer claimed to be quite the expert, and promised to teach us. He had been taking casting lessons every Sunday in the ballroom of a downtown hotel, and had acquired an expensive bamboo rod, a red neckerchief, and one of those dashing snap-brim fedoras sported by Brad Pitt in *A River Runs through It*.

The Caledon property belonged to some Canadian movie star whose name I can't recall, and the water we had permission to fish was a circular artificial pond. Fine-trimmed lawn ran down to its contoured edges, and we laid out our tackle on ornate benches. The pond had been stocked with captive rainbow trout. They had been raised on a well-balanced diet of food pellets, and we planned to slaughter them at leisure. The TV producer gave us a few basic lessons, showing us the casting strokes he'd learned in the hotel ballroom, but when he stepped up to the edge of the pond, his fly line kept snagging on the lawn behind him. Sometimes the line arced forward in a promising way then settled in festive loops on his shoulders. Paul and I eventually grew tired of watching this and decided to experiment with our own techniques. I walked to the far side of the pond and spent a long while thrashing ineffectually with the borrowed fly rod, never managing to get a fly more than a few yards beyond the shore. The sun was brutally hot and the pond seemed as lifeless as a water hazard. Down the shoreline I could see Paul having his own problems. Eventually I gave up, walked over to his side of the pond, and sat on the bench. My presence made Paul self-conscious. As the line soared back and forth in tortured loops, he grunted like a man trying to drive an axe through a chunk of elm wood. At one point, after eight or nine bullwhipping false casts, he drove the barb into the back of his vest. As I helped him remove the hook, he said, "This is demeaning."

"One thing I don't understand," I said. "Fishing is already quite difficult. Why do we have to make it more difficult by using fly rods?"

"You're saying you want to quit?"

"I'm saying I'm thirsty."

"Right," he said. He reeled in his line and waved across the pond at the TV producer. "Allan, can we go home?"

THERE ARE NO signs marking the midpoint in life. And until you spot the subtle changes in terrain, you might not even notice that you're no longer climbing. Middle age doesn't mean that your health is failing or that you're being constantly offered the senior's discount. It just means that there's now more road behind you than there is ahead, and you'd better start thinking about the places you want to see and the things you want to accomplish before the sun gets much lower in the west.

Paul and I were both dads by now, with kids and mortgages and writing careers that paid the bills. Paul the polymath was winning prizes of one kind or another with tedious regularity, and writing songs, performing with his band, and making records. When I was in Toronto, I stayed with him and his wife, Dorothy Bennie, in their comfortable house in Riverdale. I was pals with his daughters, Carson and Flannery, and we spent many an evening drawing dinosaurs at the kitchen table while the effervescent Dorothy made dinner and Paul tapped away on his laptop on the other side of the table. He had reached a stage of proficiency in which he could answer the phone and carry on conversations and work on a novel all at the same time, proving that when you've put in your ten thousand hours cutting diamonds, playing the violin, or writing stories, artistic enterprise is mainly about showing up.

Fly-fishing still eluded us though, and during long summer evening discussions in his backyard, we agreed that if we were ever going to call ourselves fishermen, we'd better get serious about the fly rod. Eventually I wangled a magazine assignment to go to the Bahamas, to write about a little island called Elbow Cay, and asked Paul to come along as my photographer. Paul knew even less about photography than I did, but he had a brand-new digital camera with a lens that deployed impressively when he pressed the buttons, and he reasoned he could study up on the basics of professional outdoor photography. The plan was, I would interview people, he would take their pictures. After I had conducted enough research to satisfy the needs of my general tourism article, we planned to sneak off for a few days and see if we could do some saltwater fly-fishing.

We flew down to Miami and caught a small plane over to the Bahamas. As our plane droned eastward across the Gulf Stream, the deep blue waters of the open sea gave way to golden islets of sand and jade-green tidal shallows. Somewhere down in those invisible shallows was one of the most elusive creatures on any fly fisherman's bucket list—the bonefish. Of the dozen-odd species that compete for the title of the World's Greatest Gamefish, the bonefish usually ranks somewhere near the top of the list. I had been studying up on the bonefish and knew a few basic facts, the main one being that they are very hard to catch. They eat shrimp, crabs, and assorted crustaceans, and while they're feeding, they keep a nervous eye peeled for their enemies—osprey, barracuda, and sharks. Because their lifestyle makes them vulnerable to predators, bonefish have developed two main defense mechanisms: constant vigilance and instant speed. A fly line looping overhead is enough to panic a whole school. But if you can get close enough, and if you can cast well enough to drop a fly into their strike zone, they're fairly indiscriminate about grabbing anything that looks like food. Once they're hooked, the payoff comes with their astounding takeoff run. According to the literature, even a small bonefish will tear off a hundred yards of line on its first sprint, and a larger one might double that. Meanwhile, if there's a flaw in your technique, reel, rod, line, or knots, the bonefish will find it for you. This was supposedly a working vacation, but as the plane cruised over all those tidal flats, I felt like we were skipping from kindergarten to graduate school.

At the north end of Abaco we caught a ferry to Elbow Cay, the last barrier island that separates the Bahamas from the open Atlantic. The ferry took us on a twenty-minute ride across the sound to Hope Town, a small New England–like fishing village with narrow streets and tiny, pastel-painted cottages. As we were hauling our bags off the ferry, we met our driver, a fiftyish, sun-bronzed white guy who introduced himself as Maitland. With his aviator sunglasses, dangling cigarette, and tough-guy accent, our driver looked like Crocodile Dundee. When he loaded our bags into the back of the van, I could see that I wasn't the first to notice the resemblance. *"Bonefish Dundee"* read the logo on the back of his T-shirt.

"My real name is Maitland Lowe," he growled. "But everyone calls me Bonefish Dundee."

As we bounced down the rough gravel road toward the hotel, I asked Maitland, "Why do they call you Bonefish Dundee?"

"Because I'm the best bonefish guide in the Bahamas."

Paul elbowed me, and looked at Maitland. "Can you take us out bonefishing?"

"Not tomorrow," he said. "I'm busy."

"And what about the next day?"

He studied us with a skeptical glance. "Can you throw a fly line?"

"We've been practicing," Paul lied.

"How do you practice in Canada in deep snow?"

"Well . . . we practiced last summer."

Maitland lit a cigarette and stared out at the road. Finally, he spat out the window and said, "I'll think about it."

Eventually we arrived at the Abaco Inn, a group of rustic cottages overlooking a deserted beach. The manager assigned us a cabin and explained that we wouldn't need a key because the island has virtually no crime. "In twenty-seven years we've never had a case of theft," she said. "The island doesn't even have a police officer."

We decided that some young Margaret Mead scholar might find good opportunity for a thesis here, comparing the sociology of Elbow Cay to nearby Miami, where you could get killed for a six-pack. By now it was late in the afternoon, so we unpacked in our cabin and went straight to the restaurant, where we ate a delicious meal of grilled grouper. After dinner, we retired to the open-air bar, where we did our best to deplete the bartender's supply of Caribbean rum. There's nothing quite as exciting as arriving in the tropics from the wintry north, so we stayed up late and closed the bar.

"I think that bartender overserved us," Paul mused as we fumbled through the velvety darkness, crashing into palm trees and tripping over rocks. It was impossibly dark, and we tugged at the door of several cabins, awaking the unfortunate tourists inside. Finally we blundered into our own tiny cabin and climbed into bed, or at least I climbed into bed. Paul started rummaging through my briefcase searching for our plane tickets. It was not clear to me why he was convinced that I'd lost the plane tickets, but he was a careful traveler and I wasn't. His job was to worry, and my job was to make him worried. Eventually he crawled into bed, fully dressed, and fell asleep. Not long afterward, I noticed that he was up again. This time he was standing in the corner, peeing on our luggage.

"Paul! Use the bathroom!"

He went into the bathroom and peed into the toilet. When he was finished, he came back and tried climbing into bed with me, with his shoes on.

The next morning, after gobbling a few aspirins and swearing off rum for the rest of our lives, we walked gingerly down to the main lodge for a bite of breakfast. Paul was chagrined to hear that he'd climbed into my bed with his shoes on, but I assured him his secret was safe with me. After munching some eggs and coffee, I took my trusty notebook and Paul took his trusty camera and we bicycled around the island, interviewing people. By mid-afternoon we'd interviewed just about everyone on the island, so we rigged up our fly rods, dragged a canoe into the water, and headed off to see if we could find some bonefish. Paul paddled while I searched the water for signs of "the ghost of the flats," then I paddled while he did the same. It was terribly hot and the sun hammered brutally on our pale northern foreheads. We kept evaluating each other's canoe-handling skills in unhelpful terms. No fish appeared. Finally we beached the canoe and decided to get into the water. Stripping down to our underwear, we waded waist-deep in the warm water for a mile or so with our fly rods. The white sand was smooth underfoot. Eventually we spotted a black stingray the size of a kitchen table. We walked right behind it for a while. It wasn't a bonefish, but Paul speculated that it might know some bonefish.

Wading half-naked for three hours without sunscreen gave us both borderline sunstroke, and I tossed in bed all night long, alternately sweating and shivering. We slept in a bit and showed up at the dining room around nine o'clock. We were halfway through our breakfast when Maitland sauntered in, lit a cigarette, and leaned up against a pillar observing us. "Well, look who's up. Do you plan to sit around all bloody morning, or do you want to go fishing?"

We gathered our tackle and hurried down to the dock, where Maitland was readying his skiff. Minutes later, we were rocketing down Abaco Sound with salty air crashing into our nostrils and the wind in our hair. As we sped along, the translucent green water and shallow bottom flashed beneath us, and shadowy fish darted away from the boat's onrushing shadow. When Maitland finally slowed down, the sun felt like a heat lamp on our bare heads. "Put on your hats, boys," he said. "It's going to be hot today."

Maitland told us that we couldn't both cast from the boat at the same time, so Paul and I flipped a coin, and I won the toss. I climbed up onto the casting platform and nervously reviewed the tips from the bonefishing books I'd studied... *Okay, shake out fifteen feet of line. Hold your fly in your rod hand. Strip off another fifteen or twenty feet and hold the coils loosely in your free hand. Now you're loaded, ready to shoot a cast at the first bonefish you see. Take a quick survey of the deck to make sure that there are no cleats or loose ropes to snag your line. Are you balanced comfortably on the balls of your feet? Are your knees slightly flexed? Look now, look ... you're standing on the line, you idiot!*

While I conducted this tense conversation with myself, Maitland unlimbered his sixteen-foot push pole. The tide was coming in, and the white-sand tidal flat was covered with transparent water. Maitland climbed up onto the platform and dug in the pole, and we glided forward. Our voices dropped to a whisper as we scanned the water around us. From the books I'd read, I knew that the first task at hand was spotting the bonefish. They're called the ghost of the flats because their chromium scales are like mirrors and enable them to disappear.

With each wisp of cloud moving across the sun, the water changed from green to turquoise to blue to green again. There was an occasional puff of silt as a stingray fled from our shadow. Farther away, I saw schools of small jacks darting past. I've always considered myself to be a half-decent spotter of birds, fish, and wildlife. But I was no match for Maitland. When I pointed to a far-off flash of movement, Maitland wouldn't even turn his head. "That's only a barracuda, sir," he said, having noticed it quite a while ago. Generally, we kept silent, and with each passing minute, the tension rose higher.

Finally a trio of fish came nosing along the bottom, headed our way. Maitland whispered, "Bonefish, eleven o'clock, sixty feet." He immobilized the boat by driving his pole into the sand, and, with my heart thudding, I made ready for the cast. My first attempt fell short, so I raised the rod for another cast. But in my haste, the line made a splash on the water and the bonefish streaked away. "Don't yank your line off the water like that," Maitland chided. "If you mess up on your first cast, strip it in gently."

Paul was generous enough to allow me another chance to screw up. After a few minutes, another trio of bonefish came along. This time my cast skidded sideways in the breeze and slapped the water about twenty feet off-target. I tried again, and a loop of line caught itself around the butt of the rod. The line was tangled. Minutes went by as Maitland glared and Paul and I frantically tried to sort out the mess. Finally we got it straightened out, and Maitland moved us forward. We had only gone a hundred feet when the boat paused. I could sense Maitland crouch like a cat on the platform. His voice was terse. "Very large bonefish right in front of you, sir. Cast quickly now, before he sees the boat."

The solitary bonefish was coming toward us, sniffing the bottom. His head was as big as a leg of lamb. I was already rattled, and the size of the fish didn't help. Rushing my cast, I snapped the line into a forward roll and fouled the hook behind me. The fish saw my arm movement and darted away. I turned around to see what I'd snagged—Maitland's wrist.

"Oh brother," I said. "Sorry about that."

He plucked the hook out. "Don't be sorry that you hooked me," he said. "Be sorry that you missed that bloody fish."

This was a disgrace. I stepped down off the platform and handed Paul the rod. "Your turn, partner."

My buck fever seemed contagious, because Paul's casting was no better than mine. Maitland maneuvered us over to the narrow entrance of a huge flat, where schools of bonefish were coming in with the flood tide, cruising past us like Manhattan taxicabs at rush hour. Paul slapped the water to the left and right, and each time he shot a cast, the water erupted with the tails of stampeded fish. He messed up every chance he got and finally handed the rod to me. "Okay, I'm tired of being the laughingstock. I want to sit and relax and smoke a cigar and laugh at *you* for a while."

"Get ready, sir," Maitland muttered. "More bonefish coming."

I was quite nervous at this point, and it didn't help that Maitland was cursing under his breath as he labored to get the heavy boat closer to the fish. My biggest fear was lining the fish, that is, casting too close and slapping the water with the line, causing the fish to panic and scare every other fish in the vicinity. I was so paranoid about lining the fish that I made sure I casted well ahead of it, which caused a paroxysm of rage and frustration in Maitland (*"You're nowhere near the bloody fish!"*). So I moved my next cast closer and dropped the line right atop the fish. When you scare one bonefish, you scare a hundred, and as my line slapped down on the fish's head, the entire glassy surface of the tidal flat erupted as if it had been blasted with a 10-gauge shotgun.

When I got to the point where I couldn't stand it anymore, I handed the rod to Paul and he took over. That's how our day went—Laurel and Hardy Go Bonefishing. At one point, a school of a hundred bonefish came cruising right toward us. It was my turn again. And although the school veered slightly, they kept coming, confident in the security of numbers. A dozen-odd fish passed us broadside, so close that a nine-year-old kid with a Pocket Fisherman could have beaned any one of them. Maddeningly, I couldn't seem to make the line work. Instead of uncoiling in graceful arcs, my fly line writhed back and forth overhead in wild snaps and finally dropped onto the water like a decapitated snake.

Oddly enough, one of the fish swam over and scoffed down the fly. I reared back on the rod and set the hook. This particular bonefish may have had a learning disability, because instead of taking on a blistering run, it swam around in confused circles. I applied pressure with the rod until it suddenly got frightened and took off. Paul and Maitland cheered. The reel screamed as the bonefish sped across the flat, but then the tension slackened and my loose fly line went racing out through the rod guides. I couldn't believe my eyes. A few days earlier, the clerk at the expensive fly-fishing store in Toronto had insisted on tying the various knots on my leader, fly line, and backing. "If you're going all the way to the Bahamas, you don't want to lose a nice fish because of a knot failure," he said.

Now my loose fly line was tearing across the water, towed by the escaping bonefish. Maitland leaped out of the boat, and galloped after it through the shin-deep water. A hundred feet from the boat, he seized the fly line and tried to hand-line the fish, but it was gone. He walked back to the boat, his face grim. "Who tied that fucking knot?"

I didn't know which was worse, saying I'd tied it myself or admitting that I'd let someone else do it. So I told him the truth, and he issued a choked laugh. Then he climbed into the boat, adjusted his baseball hat to a philosophical angle, and lit a cigarette. Losing the fish seemed to improve his mood somewhat, as if he'd finally realized that this whole undertaking was actually supposed to be a comedy. Puffing on his cigarette, he fired up the motor and told us it was quitting time. We headed back to the inn. Over the roar of the motor, Paul leaned over and asked Maitland if he wanted to fish again the next day. "No thanks," he said. "You two are hopeless."

Back at the pier, we paid him his $300 plus a large tip, and he drove off without saying a word.

That night in the bar we drank Cuba Libres and debated our next move. The bartender told us that Maitland was the only guide on the island. This was hard to understand. We had cash and we wanted to go fishing. But whatever social conditions had driven off the criminals had apparently driven off the fishing guides too. It was a beautiful night, crickets singing and palm leaves rattling in the breeze, yet we couldn't relax, being face to face with the realization that our fishing trip was turning into a rout. "Well, Paul," I finally said, slamming my glass down on the bar top. "I guess I'll have to come out of retirement."

"I beg your pardon?"

"I'm an ex–fishing guide, right? What's so complicated about it? We'll guide ourselves. We'll rent a little boat, get some maps, go back to the place that Maitland showed us, and catch some damn bonefish all by ourselves."

The next morning, we found a local marina operator who agreed to rent us a Boston Whaler. After listening to his long and confusing lecture about flare pistols, VHF emergency channels, etc., we loaded our fly rods in the boat, fired up the motor, and headed for the same place we'd fished with Maitland—Snake Cay.

When we got to Snake Cay, the tide was out, and the big bay that had been filled with shallow water the day before now looked like a mud parking lot. We waited for more than an hour, and slowly the water began to seep across the flat. But our Boston Whaler, lovely boat that it was, nevertheless drew a lot more water than Maitland's bonefish skiff. What this meant, in simple terms, was that we had to get out and push it through the shallow water, inch by inch.

It was hot, sweaty work, but we knew we deserved to be punished, and what fitter punishment than to wade through stingray-infested waters, pushing a two-thousand-pound skiff with the sun beating down on your head? We took turns pushing while the other fished. What had happened to all those bonefish? Finally I spotted a couple of dark, slow-cruising shapes in the distance and directed Paul to push us closer. "I think they're big tarpon!" I said. When we were about forty feet away, it became apparent that the two large tarpon were actually sharks, big sharks, about eight feet long. At that point Paul, out of craven self-interest, climbed into the boat, depriving me of forward power.

We fished for two days like this, without seeing a single bonefish. When we returned on our third day, we begged the bartender to tell us where Maitland lived. "We want to throw ourselves on his mercy."

It turned out that Maitland lived in a huge lemon-yellow concrete house that once belonged to the folksinger Burl Ives. The house had been damaged by the hurricane, so Maitland and his twenty-five-year-old Cuban wife were fixing it up in exchange for free rent. Obviously, Maitland wasn't rich. But this crime-free, copless island also seemed to exist apart from the normal forces of supply and demand. Ordinarily, you wave a couple of large bills in someone's face and they scurry around and do your bidding. Maitland wasn't interested in our money. "I can't be bothered taking you out," he said. "It's painful to watch."

Paul was feeling a bit offended by now, and felt that we didn't really have to stand for Maitland's contempt. "But listen, Maitland," he said, "you could be doing a better job yourself."

"How do you figure that?"

"Well, you're the guide, right? You know way more than us. Aren't you supposed to teach us? How can we learn how to cast if you don't give us some pointers?"

Maitland's face was hard and impassive.

Paul added, "You'd be a better fishing guide if you helped your guests more."

I guess no one had ever offered Maitland a critique of his guiding style. He seemed amused by Paul's nerve. "So you think I should be givin' you lessons?"

Maitland went into the house and emerged a few minutes later with a fly rod. We followed him down to the beach, where he unlimbered twenty feet of line and flipped it forward onto the water. He then peeled off a little more line and did the same again. When he was finished, he was shooting ninety feet of line, straight as an arrow, with so little effort that half an inch of ash drooped from the end of his cigarette without falling off. "You can't cast properly unless you learn to throw a straight line," he said. "Don't wiggle the rod. Slice it straight back and forth, straight on the backcast, straight on the forecast. Straight, straight, straight. Start with a short line and keep practicing until you can throw it straight. Look over your shoulder and watch your backcast. Make sure it's straight. Start with twenty feet and then twenty-five, and thirty. If you get good enough to throw a half-decent forty-foot cast, you can catch a bonefish."

"What about accuracy?" I asked.

"If you can throw it straight, you can hit anything," he said. "Watch."

He turned toward the lawn, threw a ninety-foot cast, and clipped the head off a dandelion. Then he did it again and again, yo-yoing the line back and forth, snipping the head off every dandelion within range.

"Spend the whole day casting," he said. "If you can hit a dandelion at forty feet, I'll take you out again."

That afternoon, Paul and I spent many hours on the lawn behind the inn, practicing. We cast into the wind, with the wind, and across the wind. We put bonefish-sized sticks on the grass and practiced throwing flies to them. We took turns watching each other cast, offering tips and criticism, working on the theory that it's easier to see someone else's mistakes than your own. "Watch your backcast," I kept reminding Paul. "Mind you, if I threw a backcast like that, I wouldn't want to look at it either."

"Was there a nicer way to say that?"

"Okay, you're actually doing really well."

"I don't know that I'd go that far," Maitland remarked. He had walked up to watch us without announcing himself. "But you're not as bloody awful as you were a few days ago."

After watching us for a few minutes, Maitland agreed to take us out the next day. In the morning, we woke up clear-headed and keen. We ate some breakfast, and when Maitland cruised up to the wharf, we were already waiting for him. We climbed into the boat and he hit the throttle. He looked serious, clutching the wheel with that permanent cigarette jammed in his mouth. For the better part of an hour we sped past reefs and islands and windswept rocky points. Finally we arrived at a huge, utterly desolate tidal lagoon. In the narrow entrance to the lagoon, the tide boiled and swirled like a jungle river. And as we trolled through the rocky entrance, a pair of carpet-sized eagle rays swam under the boat. A few minutes later, Maitland cruised into a wide, white-sand flat covered with Jello-green water. He had no sooner deployed his push pole than we saw a school of bonefish—sixty or eighty of them, swimming along the beach with their backs out of the water. On Maitland's directions, Paul jumped out of the boat and began stealthily wading toward them. I got up on the casting platform in case we spotted some others.

Maitland pushed the boat in a different direction so that we wouldn't spoil Paul's stalk. We hadn't gone more than fifty feet when four large bonefish appeared out of nowhere, headed right toward us. Reminding myself to let the line straighten out and load up properly on my backcast, I accidentally shot a perfect cast. The fly touched the water and settled, and the largest fish approached the fly and sniffed it like a dog. I felt the faintest tug on the line (I'd rehearsed all this in my imagination a hundred times) and then I executed a strip strike in approved Bonefish Dundee fashion, tugging on the line and then raising the rod tip in a sweeping strike. In response, the rod suddenly jumped to life. The reel exploded into a frenzied scream and Maitland issued a rebel yell. "You got him!"

That first run must have lasted thirty seconds, with the reel howling and Maitland shouting at me to hold the rod tip high. The rod was bent flat and the line continued tearing off until the fish was far out of sight. When it was perhaps two hundred yards across the lagoon, it made a right turn and sprinted the other way, and Maitland warned me again to keep the rod high so that the long line wouldn't snag on a coral outcrop. "I love that sound, sir," Maitland said over the crazed whirring of the reel. "All this work, all these years of chasing bonefish—I do it just so that I can hear that sound."

Five minutes into the fight, the bonefish made a hard turn and we spotted a shark chasing it. Maitland jumped out of the boat with a gaff hook and galloped toward the shark, swinging the gaff and swearing. The shark took off in a cloud of silt, and for the next while, I just kept the rod tip high and tried to avoid making any mistakes. The fish was swimming in ever-smaller circles, and my arms were getting rubbery from the nonstop isometric pull of the rod. It was twenty minutes on Maitland's wristwatch when the fish finally glided into his hands. I jumped into the water and lifted it, a dense creature, heavy as a silver ingot, with blue iridescence flashing off its skin. "Thanks, Maitland," I said. "Nice coaching."

"Beautiful fish," said Maitland. "Eight pounds. Very nice for your first one."

Kneeling down in the tepid water, I moved the fish back and forth until its tail began to work. After a moment or two it swam away. I washed my hands and climbed back into the boat.

"Let's go," said Maitland. "It looks like your buddy needs help."

I looked across the flat at Paul. He was knee-deep in water, yelping in celebration. His rod was bent over and his line was throwing a shear of water as his bonefish sped across the flat.

That was our initiation as fly fishermen, and over the next fifteen years we fished all over the place—New Brunswick, Quebec, northern Ontario, rural Manitoba, the Alberta foothills, the Queen Charlottes, the coastal rivers of British Columbia, the Florida Keys, the mangrove flats of Cuba, both coasts of Mexico, and all over the Bahamas. We fished in so many beautiful places that it would make a good Hank Snow song. We froze our fingers walleye fishing in blowing snow, and we rode out a mini hurricane in the Gulf Stream, with sideways rain and lightning bolts smacking the water all around us. We once spent an afternoon on a Bahamian island that was so peaceful and idyllic that we actually stopped fishing for a while as Paul uneasily put forward the proposition that maybe, just maybe, our airplane had crashed and we'd been killed and this in fact was Heaven.

Between fishing trips we spent many hundreds of hours practicing with our fly rods, clipping dandelions and trying to throw arrow-string casts. We practiced in the wind, the damned wind, and debated different theories of the cast. We worked on our timing and muscle memory. We practiced separately and we practiced together. After an endless amount of practice we became good enough that we were almost competent. When we met a new fishing guide, he would ask us to peel off some line and throw a practice cast or two. Watching us fling sixty feet of crooked line across the water, he'd grunt quietly and say, "Okay, you'll do."

We sat in countless airports and roomed together and got to know each other's quirks. After a number of years, fishing buddies become like an old married couple, with the same long catalogue of inside jokes and petty grievances. Paul could be cranky and vague. He was a silent worrier, always checking his watch and patting his pockets. I teased him about it, but he pointed out that if our travel schedule had been left up to me, we would have ended up practicing our knots in the airport departure lounge while the plane took off without us. Friendship between men is usually considered to be an uncomplicated arrangement, filled with lots of straight talk and hearty laughter, but Paul and I were never comfortable together. We found friendship to be a difficult undertaking, like fly-fishing. We did fine when we were out in a boat, fishing, but when it was just the two of us, sitting at a dinner table or in a bar, we just kind of sat there and looked at each other. I always wondered what that awkwardness meant. Certain things remained unsaid, mainly because we didn't know what to say. Maybe we were just typical men, and felt uncomfortable sitting face to face. Maybe he thought I didn't respect him, and vice versa. It troubles me to admit it, but the competitiveness between us sometimes set the tone. I sometimes hinted that his writing was overpraised, and I can still see the hurt and surprise on his face when I once addressed him as "fatboy." After a drink or two I enjoyed having sport with him in front of other fishermen. He accused me of stealing his jokes and cozying up to guides so I could play two-against-one. He wrote a couple of fishing books in which he gave rather one-sided versions of the many small indignities he'd suffered at my hands.

Sometimes it felt like our shared interest in fishing was the only slender thread holding us together.

One day we were fishing in Minaki and I noticed he was coughing a lot. I chastised him about smoking cigars, but he said they kept him warm. A few months later he was playing poker with his buddies in Toronto and they also chided him about his smoking. "They were joking that I probably have lung cancer," he told me on the phone. "Which they seemed to think was funny."

I told Paul he might have blastomycosis, a rare lung infection unique to northwestern Ontario. "Most doctors won't know what it is. So you have to tell him you were fishing out here at my cottage, and he has to research it. Fishermen and forestry workers and people like that are susceptible. It's quite treatable, but you need the proper diagnosis."

Paul was encouraged by this news. A few days later I was in Toronto and he came to pick me up in his Subaru wagon. It was a very hot day in May. We drove around looking for a place to have lunch. Paul seemed fixated on the idea of having lunch at a strip bar. We ended up driving around in the industrial wasteland out near the airport, and parked next to a low-slung concrete building advertising Naked Women Cold Beer. The interior of the bar was gloomy and deserted. Up on the small neon-lit stage, a thick-waisted, naked, and rather homely woman from Colombia or some war-torn country was shaking her booty. Paul and I ordered drinks and sat there looking at each other. "So how did the meeting with the doctor go?" I asked.

"The doctor was proud to report that he knew all about blastomycosis. He says, 'Oh no, you don't have blasto. I know all about blasto because I worked in the Kenora Health Unit for a couple of years.'"

"Oh yeah, what's the guy's name?"

Paul told me his name.

"I don't know him."

"Yeah, so he told me all about his happy days working in Kenora and all his fishing trips on the Lake of the Woods and on and on..." Paul took a sip of his beer. We were ignoring the naked fat girl, but Paul seemed content with the surroundings. I think he wanted a stripper present for this conversation.

"So what else did he say?"

"Well, I finally interrupted his nostalgic monologue and said, 'Well, Doc, if I don't have blasto, what do I have?'"

"'Oh,' he says, 'you have Stage Four lung cancer.' I says, 'So how serious is it?' He says, 'Well, put it this way, there's no Stage Five.'"

Somehow I wasn't surprised, but it was a hard thing to hear. "Is it treatable?"

"'Well,' he says, 'unfortunately your type of cancer is not operable, and is usually terminal within the year.'"

We talked about it for another few minutes. I told him about people I knew who had experienced miraculous recoveries from cancer, and Paul said, "I want to be one of those people." But it seemed odd that there was so little to say. We spend all our lives waiting for the dragon to stagger into our path. When it finally does, there's not a lot to say. Disease in any form turns out to have limited conversational potential, and cancer is, of all things, boring.

The news came as a shock to everyone who knew Paul. Sympathy calls poured in, and Paul embarked on a hyperactive program of writing and musical creativity. I felt guilty about my underperformance as a friend, and offered to fly out to Toronto and keep him company. He was still quite healthy at this point; everyone focused on the possibility that he might be one of those freak individuals who live for a dozen or more years after a bad diagnosis. He had bought his own houseboat by now and kept it in a marina over on the Toronto Islands. It was a great clumsy beast the size of a Winnebago, and on warm summer evenings we cruised around the back bays, casting flies from the high roof and trying not to collide with other boaters.

Finally, as fall approached, we decided to take one last fishing trip to the Bahamas, during which I planned to have "a good talk" with my old fishing partner. It wasn't clear what we'd talk about, but that was my plan. In anticipation of our trip, he would phone me from the road, affecting that stagy Arkansas drawl he would drop into when we talked about going fishing. "When are y'all thinking we're gonna take this here bucket trip?"

But the disease was moving quickly. He collapsed on tour, and afterward he had to wheel an oxygen tank with him everywhere. By December it was a challenge just crossing the street, let alone navigating big airports or wading on a bonefish flat. I spent many nights lying awake, regretting my inability to do anything useful and wondering what I could do to repair all those years of petty rivalry. I felt like I had to say something to him, but what? Something had gone unstated in our near lifelong conversation, but I wasn't sure what it was.

Finally, in January, I decided to fly out to Toronto and have a confessional talk with him, in which I intended to ask his forgiveness—for the jibes, the dismissive comments, the disrespect, and all the times I had made sport of his failures and ignored his successes. I wanted to tell him I was grateful for all the good travels we'd had together, and I wanted to tell him how lucky I'd been to have him as a friend. I bought a ticket to arrive on Thursday and planned to go out on the town with him on Friday night. It was a good plan, but my timing was off. On Wednesday night, as I was packing my bags to come and see him, he took an extra dose of painkiller to help him through the night, fell asleep, and never woke up.

Our Friday-night outing turned out to be a wake. I attended but Paul didn't. Hundreds of his friends and acquaintances crowded into a blues bar. The female vocalist for his band, Rebecca Campbell, came up to me in the crowd. She had logged years on the road with Paul and the other members of his band, the Porkbelly Futures. Paul and Rebecca had talked about every imaginable subject as the miles rolled by, and had come to know each other as only traveling companions can. I told Rebecca that my one major regret was that Paul and I had never had our big talk. She seized me by the arm, almost fiercely, and looked me in the eye. "That guy really loved you," she said. "Do you know that?"

It wasn't much of a consolation. But in the end, it was the one thing I needed to know.

Fish out of Water

DAVID CARPENTER

A version of this essay was previously published in Numéro Cinq.

ONE JUNE MORNING in 1968, while wrestling with a stump, my father had a heart attack. He was sixty-two. My mother packed him into the car and drove him to the hospital. That night she phoned and told me to meet her at the cardiac ward the next morning. I saw her standing just outside his room. She had spotted me coming down the corridor, and when we made eye contact, she shook her head. *No,* she seemed to say, *he might not make it.*

Dr. Flanagan had a different take on Dad's condition.

"Your father is very lucky we got to him when we did." A moment later he added, "But yes, your father is a very sick man." I tried to put this very bad, good news together: a not-yet-fatal massive heart attack. The next week would be crucial in determining his chances for recovery. Dad wanted to talk but could scarcely whisper. I knelt down to hear him.

"It's amazing," he said, "in here, how they fix you up."

We visited with Dad and consulted with his team, and I wrote to my brother not to worry; there was nothing he could do but wait for further developments.

The doctors claimed that Dad was stable, and he did seem to be rallying in small ways. After a few days of guarded hopes and worried looks, my mum said, "You may as well go fishing with your friends. Not much is going to happen this weekend."

THERE IS A cabin belonging to the Anderson family that sits on the shores of Lake Edith, which in turn lies almost in the shadow of Pyramid Mountain in the heart of Jasper National Park. At one end of the lake, a small feeder stream winds through the gloom of a forest of ferns, thick bush, muskeg, and Douglas fir. It bubbles up from beneath the massive roots of an old fir and murmurs its way over the gravel and into Lake Edith. The lake is shaped like a pair of sunglasses, seen front-on, and it would have been two small lakes but for the presence of a shallow channel connecting the bodies of water. The water is absolutely clear. From the shallows to the depths, this lake covers the spectrum from pale green to near purple. The rainbows that spawn in the tiny stream and in the spring-fed beds of gravel out on the lake are pampered by a sumptuous array of nymphs, bugs, and minnows. The rainbows of Lake Edith, when I was a young fly-fishing fool, grew bigger and fatter than any other trout in the park. Right at sundown the big ones would cruise the shallows for emerging insects a few yards from shore. The water is so clear and placid in the evening that you could see them coming a block away.

MY FATHER WAS a practical man and a family man. He never crossed the line on such things as drunkenness, womanizing, gambling, or anything of an addictive nature. He taught me and my brother about fishing, but he could never have predicted how easily I would become addicted to fly-fishing. I read *Outdoor Life* and *Field & Stream* and stocking stats and fishing guides with the devotion of a literary scholar. Writers like Roderick Haig-Brown and Izaak Walton had conversations with me in my dreams.

On the subject of politics, my father always said, *Don't get carried away*. On the subject of idealistic quests, my father said, *Don't get carried away*. On the subject of various girls, he said, *Don't get carried away*. On the subject of anything bohemian and free-spirited (which included playing the banjo), my father said, *Don't get carried away*. Even on the subject of fly-fishing, he said, *Don't get carried away*. On the subject of saving my money for a rainy day, however, he would say, *Now you're talkin, son*.

I learned how to cast flies with my friend Hyndman one winter when I was fifteen. Every Wednesday night we would take a long bus ride to a school in Edmonton's east end. There we would practice casting under the tutelage of an old Highlander, whipping flies beneath basketball hoops at target patterns on the gym floor. Our guru never tired of telling us, *Laddie, y'kenna catch a fesh if yer line's no in the water.* By the end of the winter we could cast a straight line forty feet or more and tie a few basic flies. I remember a streamer we called the Kilburn Killer, named after a man in our club, which imitated a minnow about two inches long.

My father paid for it all. My first fly rod, my subscription to *Outdoor Life*, and my membership in the Edmonton fly-fishing club. *Have fun, but don't get carried away.* At fifteen years, I was the monster he created. Thank God, my friend Hyndman was just as obsessive as I was.

THE ANDERSONS' CABIN at Lake Edith was a social, psychological, spiritual, piscatorial, culinary smorgasbord of conviviality. When I arrived on the evening of opening day (always June 15 in Jasper Park), Lynn Anderson (lean, tall, a hiker, incurably sociable) threw open the door. The Youngbloods were urging all the peoples of the world to get together, and everybody in the room was dancing. We were in our twenties. Lynn and I were schoolteachers. She had yet to become a full-time artist, her boyfriend, Lloyd, had yet to become a lawyer, and I had yet to become a writer. Anything was possible. That's what the Youngbloods were telling us as we danced. That's what the wine was telling us, what the month of June was telling us, what my father's bout with mortality was telling us: Life, opportunity, and Suzie Q were ours for the asking. We were, I am sure, getting carried away.

The plan was to party till four or five in the morning and then hit the lake. There would be a prize for the biggest rainbow. Perhaps only a few of us took the contest seriously, but I was one of them. My archrival in this endeavor was Scot Smith, another victim of fly-fishing addiction.

Maybe a dozen of us left the party before dawn and went down to the water to cast from shore or troll from the Andersons' canoe or fish from some other boat. The water was calm and so was the fishing, and then the sun rose, the insects in the shallows got going, and Scot had a hit, and Lloyd got a hit, and one of Lynn's brothers got a hit, and I got a hit, and all over the lake, eager voices, mostly male, were calling out, *I got one* or *I lost the (expletive) fish* or *I just saw a monster* or *you've just crossed my (expletive) line again* or *I got another one.*

By late morning, Lynn was barbecuing a rainbow that was, if I remember correctly, just shy of five pounds. It was one of Scot's fish, and the bar for the biggest trout had been set.

One by one, weary anglers all over the lake retired to their sleeping bags and their cabin bunks, and when at last I brought in a 5-pounder and claimed the prize, Scot was the only angler from our party left out on the water. Before long, perhaps late in the afternoon, he came in with a fat silver rainbow so clearly bigger than mine that I knew my labors had only just begun. I grabbed my waders and set out for the other side of the lake, the shaded end where the little feeder stream flowed in, wearing for itself a shallow channel that dropped steadily off into the deep water where the lake followed the spectrum from pale green to blue to purple.

This was where the last of the ragged ones patrolled the shoreline. The spring spawn was over now, so these were legal to catch. Their numbers had dwindled to about a dozen from more than a hundred. When I arrived, these last fish were nosing through the shallows like the last revelers to leave a party. They made half-hearted runs at their rivals and continued to circle past the redds as though caught up and exhausted by the perplexing mysteries of love that the Youngbloods still sing about.

No fish remained in the feeder stream. The rainbows in the shallows were rolling past in about three feet of water in front of me. They seemed to prefer the gravel here to that in the little stream, where they would have been vulnerable to predators. They all looked pretty big to me, but one dark male seemed longer than any other fish in that exhausted band of spawn-fraught rainbows.

I waded in and stripped some line from my reel.

It is fun to imagine my father watching this moment of intense concentration from the beach, or reading this little adventure of mine in a magazine. He would approve. He would say, *That's real living, son*. He wasn't exactly mad about my books. My writing about self-deluded drunks, gay librarians, libidinous women, doomed victims, godless womanizers, and criminals probably left him wondering where he had gone wrong. These things were absolutely un-Carpenterian. But writing about the sporting life was okay with Paul Carpenter. It was something he could show his friends without embarrassment. He was like most fathers of his generation. He wanted his son to have a good job, a good marriage, and if he had to do this writing stuff, let it be a hobby. Let's not get carried away.

A few of my friends from that summer were married, and most of them were paired off and likely entering their own bouts of intense spawning with their partners, so the month of June, up at Lake Edith, had for them, even more than me, a sweet and urgent tumescence with which the rainbow trout, decked in their deepest greens, reds, pinks, and blues, seemed in tune. Or no, perhaps it was the other way around: my friends, besotted in deepest desire, were in tune with all those pink-sided Cupids sweeping their tails in slow, exhausting circles over the gravel beds and every so often thrusting their bodies into the silted bottom of Lake Edith.

Why did I do this? Was winning a prize for the biggest fish so important that I would disturb this last bout of spawning? Was this done for bragging rights? Or, in the absence of any spawning in my own life, was I simply sublimating into something over which I had some control? Socially, at that time, and sexually, romantically, I was a fish out of water.

Enough of that.

I waded as close as I dared to the action before me and sent out a cast that went beyond the school of circling trout.

All day long I had been thinking about my gray-faced father in his bed in the cardiac ward, and how surprised he would be at the sight of a huge trout. I would catch it for him. Well, no, I would catch a big one for me and then *present* it to him. He'd get a kick out of it and maybe stop looking quite so gray. I wanted my father to be proud of me.

And I was getting carried away. When you want your father to be proud of you, you are probably wading through uncertain waters and unlikely to inspire pride in anyone—until you get over this need to impress him.

I let my line sink to the sandy bottom and began a slow retrieve. The fly I had chosen was my big, self-tied Kilburn Killer, a streamer fly I've never seen in a store. It plowed through the sand and gravel like a somnolent minnow with a death wish, an inebriate who showed up at the wrong party and risked becoming part of the menu.

When the great dark rainbow came back my way, I pulled the streamer up from the gravel and drew it toward me in short, irregular jerks. The big rainbow went right for it. I spotted the white interior of his opening mouth as he snapped at my fly; I raised the rod, and he was on. He bucked around in slow motion, sending the other fish outward from the spawning trenches in a wide explosion of silt. He moved off to my right, changed directions, flopped around, kicked up a mighty spray with his tail, and took off for deep waters.

"Verrrry nice," someone said.

I didn't recognize the voice and I didn't dare turn around. Perhaps he was a cabin owner or a conservation officer. I heard the click of a camera, an authoritative slide of the shutter. It was an expensive sound.

The old rainbow fought stubbornly, but never once did he jump out of the water or do a high-speed run to take my ratchet into the upper registers.

"If I had a cottage on this lake," the voice said, "I would *not* go swimming out there. Not with guys like *that* in the neighborhood."

"He's a big one," I said to the voice.

It did not sound like a fisherman's voice. It was lisping and pedantic, and mildly sarcastic even when opportunities for sarcasm were unavailable.

"Rots a ruck, buddy."

This is the point in the story where the angler gazes down on the dark blue-green back, the wide band of deepest rose on the side, flecked with dark spots from head to tail, and sees his fly protruding from the corner of the kipe jaw, and he is overwhelmed by the beauty of the old trout. He bends down, detaches his fly. He holds the trout by the tail and moves its body back and forth, opening and closing the gill covers, reviving his old adversary, and sends him back to spawn again.

That didn't happen. I brained the old rainbow with a piece of wood and held him up for inspection.

"Do you think you could kind of clean it up for me?"

I looked into the face of a man with a notebook. The mystery voice with the Daffy Duck intonations belonged to a newspaper reporter. Another man, a quiet fellow with a camera, stood beside him.

These two had come all the way from Edmonton to cover opening day for the sports page of the *Edmonton Journal*. The cameraman shot me and my trout from several more angles while the man with the notebook asked me questions. And then, with a rush of purest joy and more than a trace of vanity, I knew how I would give my father a boost.

MUM WAS SITTING in a chair by Dad's bed, reading a section of the newspaper and occasionally looking over in Dad's direction. He had gone through the front section and the business reports and the editorials and made it at last to the sports page. He pulled a straight pin from the top pocket of his hospital gown and began to cut out an article. Did other people's fathers do this? I don't know. He handed the article to Mum with the usual comment.

"Something for the boys."

My mother perused the picture and the article, which she had already read, and handed it back to my father.

"Remind you of someone?" she said.

Perhaps my father's eyesight had been affected by the heart attack, or perhaps he hadn't been wearing his glasses. Or perhaps he was still preoccupied with his own mortality. But perhaps, as well, at this moment my dad would have heard a note of mischief in my mother's voice. He looked once more at the trout in the photo and this time he read the photo caption.

"As I live and breathe."

As I live and breathe. Coming from a man who was so recently on the critical list, these words seemed well chosen. Dad's recovery dates from the day he saw a picture of his son in the *Edmonton Journal*. It's one thing, I guess, to catch a big fish; it's quite another thing to have it celebrated for all to see.

I HAD DECIDED on the shores of Lake Edith that Dad needed a homecoming gift. I took my frozen rainbow to a taxidermist. The process took longer than expected, so I presented my trophy to Dad on his birthday, more than a month after he'd returned from the hospital. It was attached to an oval mount made of stained maple, a twenty-seven-inch stuffed male with all the original spawning colors shamelessly enhanced by the taxidermist. Mum and Dad decided to hang it in the den.

A time came when my parents sold their home in Alberta and retired to the gentler climate of British Columbia's coast. They had to downsize drastically, so they gave me back my rainbow trophy. They did this rather easily, as though the value I had attached to the stuffed fish was in excess of their own sentiments. This makes sense to me now, because if Dad had caught the rainbow and presented it to me while I was convalescing, I might do the same.

I hid the stuffed rainbow in the basement of my house in Saskatoon. I suppose I did not want anyone to think that I made trophies from the fish I caught. It seemed, by that time, disrespectful to the fish.

Honor Kever, my girlfriend, a visual artist, agreed. She was drawn to my little family saga of Dad and the mounted rainbow, and she decided to photograph it. She arranged her shots in the following way: Shot #1, the head of my fish just up to the gills; Shot #2, the tail of my fish; both shots in black and white. She framed the head shot on the left side of my study window and the tail shot on the right side. Missing in the middle, of course, was the body of the fish. An entire window separated the head from the tail.

One winter night in early 1985, Honor said, "Why not return your fish to that feeder stream?"

At first this suggestion seemed like a bleeding-heart gesture. But the more I thought about her idea, the more it gained an aura of atonement, and it took hold. The following August, we drove west to the Rockies and found a motel in the Jasper townsite. The next morning, we drove out to Lake Edith, and for the first time, Honor saw the Anderson cabin, the view of Pyramid Mountain, the two sections of the lake, and the small feeder stream.

There were very few people around the lake, and no evidence of fish. The park had stopped stocking many years earlier. Only a very small population of trout remained, perhaps the progeny of those few that had managed to spawn uninterrupted in or near the feeder stream.

Honor and I had work to do. The light was fading rapidly, as it does this far north in late August. We had brought a hammer and a sturdy five-inch nail. We rolled a large log over to a tree we had selected, a black spruce that perched above the feeder stream. I climbed onto the log so that my boots were a good three feet off the ground. Then I detached the trout from its maple mount and drove the spike through the middle of the trout and into the spruce tree. We rolled the log away, and as Honor photographed my rainbow in his tree, I had a last look at him. He was drifting above his creek, pointed upstream toward the pure source of his water.

I was thinking about my father, the man who taught me to fish but who never made the time to learn fly-fishing. He had taken me and my friend Hyndman fishing on many occasions when he might more happily have lazed around the backyard, resting from his labors. Now he was an old man living with his wife far from the prairie of his youth, and unaware of this hairbrained scheme cooked up by my girlfriend and me. My dad, who didn't die that year after all, who lasted many more years. I was thinking that this was an appropriate ending to the story—the sound of Honor's camera reminding me of that other camera two decades ago.

A STORY DOESN'T end until someone writes it down. Honor and I got married in 1990. I had lost that fish-out-of-water feeling of being the odd man out. Oh yes, and she loves to fly-fish.

It was time for my annual drive out to British Columbia to see my parents in their apartment. To get there, we had to go through Jasper, so once again we got a motel room and went for a drive near Lake Edith. A man was fishing close to the feeder stream, and he noticed Honor and me looking for our old friend the rainbow up in his tree.

We found the black spruce that had been his resting place, and the spike that had impaled him up there, but the rainbow was gone. We approached the angler, who was not a tourist but a local man.

"Bet I know what you was lookin for."

"What?" said Honor.

"You was lookin for that Jesus big fish."

We played dumb. "What fish would that be?" I said.

"Up there, over there, used to be a old rainbow trout, nailed to the tree. Huge thing." He spread out his hands in that hyperbolic way of anglers. "No guff, it was three foot long. Musta weighed twenny pounds."

Six pounds would be closer to the mark, several ounces lighter than Scot Smith's biggest rainbow from the summer of '68. From having recently spawned, mine was a lean fish.

The man reeled in a gob of worms and a bobber and checked his bait for signs of predatory behavior. Then he stood and launched his wormy delight far out into the lake.

"Yessir, they're in here."

Playing dumb to the end, I asked him, "How did this monster fish get up in a tree?"

"They say it was some kind of a . . . like a totem, eh? Indian guy?"

I asked him where the fish was now.

"No one knows," the man said, lounging next to his cooler. "Figure somebody took it." He looked up at me. "For luck, eh?"

I still have Honor's black and white photographs, the ones of the tail and the head, separated by the window in my study. It's the big space in between that draws your attention and invites you to imagine just how big that trout was. So it's no longer a trophy, a vanity, a thing to make my father proud of me.

It's just a reminder now of that summer when my dad looked over the edge but didn't get carried away.

Live Water Dying

BY ANNIE PROULX

THOSE OF US who fish the same water year after year are tempted to say that we "know" a stream or river, for in our comparatively short lifetimes these rivers seem immutable: we know they are ancient, with histories that extend deep into the pre-human past of glaciers, prolonged droughts, searing volcanic heat, and drowned dinosaurs. Rivers, like forests, are alive and responsive to invisible and seemingly quixotic forces. Today we know that dammed reservoirs are significant sources of methane emissions and that live, running streams and rivers are vitally important in sequestering carbon. Fishermen, already excellent observers of the processes of nature, have a front-row seat to observe how the rivers they know mutate with climate change. The observation post is as near as one's favorite live-water fishing stream.

145

I have lived and fished for years on a mile of a beautiful Wyoming river at an elevation a little under 7,000 feet. I can look south to the Sierra Madres, look east and see the Medicine Bows. These two ranges are the sources of the North Platte, home to browns, rainbows, and cutthroats. The river is almost totally dependent on the annual Rocky Mountain snowpack for the rich, cold water that sustains its heavy fish. It is a handsome freestone river, still mostly wild in the high country near its source, and clean. Its northern reaches attract knowledgeable and serious fishermen. These waters are classic trout habitat, with deep green-gold pools, riffles over trout-colored boulders, swift runs, and sheltered pockets.

If any entity can claim to "know" this river, it is the bald eagles who make their living on it. One eagle family lives near our house, its nest above a long riffle that drops into a pool. The young practice their first fishing efforts by standing on the edge of a gravel bar and waiting for dinner to swim by. Several years ago, one of the adult eagles, who wade the shallows or swoop down from above, got its talons into a trout too large to lift and rode it downstream like a trick rider on a half-broke bronco, finally guiding it into the shallows.

A PHOTOGRAPH BY the pioneer Wyoming photographer J. E. Stimson shows an angler standing on the rocky shore and tussling with a big one. The place he stands is a few hundred yards from where our house stands today. Very little seems to have changed. Even the boulders and the cottonwoods on the bank look identical. The photograph was published in a 1910 issue of *The Outing Magazine* to illustrate a bombastic article titled "The Greatest Trout-Fishing Town in the World," by Charles E. Van Loan. The article plays up the gigantic local fish festival featuring an unbridled assault on the river's famed pools. For years the local people annually caught up to four thousand pounds of trout in two or three days for this tourist festival.

Those greedy times, so reminiscent of the white settlers' "wasty ways" scorned by Nathanial Hawthorne's Natty Bumppo, are gone forever. Still, the density of fish population in this section of the river is four thousand to six thousand per mile. If I stand on top of the 500-foot cliff on the north side, I can look down and see fish in the river as the eagle sees them. Many are large, certainly over four pounds. And if I stand on the bank below in the place the angler stood in that old photograph, I can compare today's reality with the scene captured more than a century ago. The river in the photograph looks wider and deeper, and this may be no trick of the eye. Climate change is working on this river.

Wyoming is a dry place, with an average precipitation of just fourteen to sixteen inches a year. The state is exquisitely sensitive to moisture variations, and variation is the name of the current game. Wyoming is also infamously windy; evaporation tends to suck up rain and snow before the drops or flakes hit the ground. The vital snowpack accumulates in the mountains above 10,000 feet, but less than 10 percent of the state's surface geography is at that elevation. Every wild creature depends on the slow-melting snowpack to live, especially cold-water-loving trout, which prefer water temperatures in the 50s Fahrenheit. When the water goes above 72° Fahrenheit, trout begin to die.

In the winter of 2010–2011, the winter snowpack was immense. The snow kept coming and coming, piling up into massive drifts. Everyone knew that when the river crested in June 2011, it would be a monster. The town prepared for a massive inundation with sandbags, and the National Guard stood ready; householders along the river began to bite their nails. And it came, the worst flood since 1917. More severe and more frequent flooding is one of the markers of a warming climate. Seven miles from town, we had more than enough water thanks to beaver dams on the tributary, Jack Creek, which jumped its banks and inundated low ground. The North Platte spread itself out and fish swam over our garden. Forty acres of sagebrush, which cannot stand water, died. Massive cottonwoods roaring downstream lodged along the shore, and driftwood floated two hundred feet inland. When the water receded weeks later, we found Game & Fish signs, a crushed canoe, fence posts in the woods, and tons of fine sand and shell deposits. The main river had seized the chance to remake its bed, erasing many gravel bars familiar to fishermen, piling up others in strange and awkward arrangements. Fishermen who thought they knew every hole and bar on the river discovered they now knew nothing at all. At our section of the river, an enormous cottonwood hulk floated onto the end of our island, where it stayed and acted as a partial dam. In the channel behind this dam, the river gouged out a small deep pool about thirty feet across. This lovely little pool, which did not exist before the flood, now has a tenant; a fisherman saw an enormous brown trout in it this past summer. He described it by holding his hands eight inches apart and saying, "It was *this* wide." Useless to speculate on its length or weight.

The heavy snow and flood that year pleased the people denying global warming—for them it was proof the place was not getting warmer and drier... until the next year came. That winter of 2011–2012 very little snow fell. The snowpack was pathetic, and in spring and summer, Wyoming, like the surrounding states, suffered shocking heat and drought, the cool mountain air of yesteryear burned away. The North Platte went down and down, turning into a long, twisted, bony trickle. The water was warm—*too* warm. Fishing was bad. The trout took refuge in the deepest pools and stayed there. When water temperatures crept up to 73° Fahrenheit in August, neighboring state Montana closed some of its streams and Yellowstone Park closed the Madison, Gallatin, and Firehole rivers. Our river stayed open, but the fishing was poor.

We know that Wyoming's temperature is rising despite its high elevation. The historical average is based on temperatures from the hundred-year period 1900 to 2000. In the years from 2003 to 2007 alone, the state became two degrees warmer than the old average. The spring melt comes earlier; the seasonal arrival and departure times of the birds that breed along the river seems to be shifting. Many fishing guides, fishermen, tourism promoters, and townspeople in fishing communities prefer to think the warm years are anomalies. But what if they aren't? What is going to happen to trout fishing on the North Platte?

Among the dozens of studies on the effect of climate change on regional fishing rivers are several unpalatable predictions for the North Platte. As temperatures increase, cold-water species will be pushed north and warm-water species will move in. Northern rivers in general will likely get more precipitation in the winter because of warmer temperatures, but that will cause heavier runoff and more erosion, meaning more chemicals from agricultural lands, more heavy metals from old mine tailings, and soil from steep mountain slopes that recently lost their lodgepole pine forests to beetle kill. Heavier discharge also means more silt and sand will be carried into the live water, limiting the amount of sunlight that can reach the bottom of the river, causing changes in plant growth and increasing soil and gravel deposition.

The earlier melting of the snowpack, the earlier cresting of the river, and the earlier start of low-water conditions all will change the habitats of water plants, fish, and other aquatic creatures that have adapted to the very specific low-flow conditions of the past. And in periods of extended low river flow, trout survival rates drop.

Scientists tell us these things, but for fishermen who are intimately involved in this ancient blood sport of fishing, the question of what to do becomes personal. As landowners on good trout water, we encouraged the growth of willows and cottonwoods along the shore to create shady fish retreats. We wrapped hundreds of mature cottonwoods with heavy wire to deter beaver cutting. Beaver, unfortunately, will gnaw themselves out of habitat and then move on. Nor did we fish when the temperatures moved into the 70s Fahrenheit. A stream thermometer was a must.

Although I am not one for organizations and clubs, many fishing societies are working to increase spawning opportunities by bringing down old dams and protecting what is left of the cold trout water. Anglers can make a difference by learning what climate change is doing to their cold-water rivers, and helping any small way they can to keep wild fish alive in their native wild rivers.

There is little doubt that new weather patterns are emerging. Just a few weeks ago in June 2014 the North Platte flooded again—the third major flood in five years. Local river watchers are thinking this is the new normal, not a hundred-year event. Once more the gravel bars are shifting, the already extensive bar between the two bridges in the town of Saratoga is extending north. My geologist friend Dave Quitter said, "You can see it in the mountains. Because of the beetle-kill deforestation, there are steeper drops for the snow melt. Some gradients that were thirty degrees a few years ago are now eighty degrees." For fishermen on this river, it will be like coming into new, unknown country.

More Than Just a Sport

WAYNE CURTIS

I COME FROM a long line of river people: boat pilots, log driv-
ers, stuntmen, cabin builders, outfitters, canoeists, guides,
and anglers. We have been living on the Miramichi for two
hundred years, seven generations. All of my forebears have
been able of soul and body, and all have been blessed with
the genes of longevity.

My great-great-grandfather John Curtis came here from
England in 1818, and swam the river at the Strawberry
Marsh to meet his awaiting bride.

David Curtis, his son, was a lumberman and a riverboat
pilot on the *Andover,* a stern-wheeler that plied our river in
the 1860s and '70s. Great-Grandfather knew every bar and
boulder on the Miramichi which could be navigated, except,
of course, in the upper reaches, where the water was shallow.
It was said of Grandfather David that he was so strong, he

would put a barrel of flour under each arm and carry them up a steep hill from the boat, to a store or farmhouse. During lumber booms, he carried logs from the big truck-wagons and loaded the tall ships moored at the wharves in Newcastle. David married Elizabeth Harris, of Jewish descent, and they raised nine children.

I have only seen one photograph of the old man. It was taken in 1938, when he was a century old. His shoulders were sloped from many decades of carrying cargo; he had a long, flowing beard and resembled Leonardo da Vinci's depiction of the apostle Paul. It was said that at the age of 103, Great-Grandfather died while sitting on the front porch, reading a Bible without glasses, and smoking his pipe. Having had his first taste of chewing tobacco at age three, he joked, he had abused the substance for over a hundred years. They said, "Father would have lived to be an old man had he been able to kick his tobacco habit."

My grandfather Tom ("Papa"), his son, was born in December of 1870. He was a log driver, a stuntman, and a scrapper. As an adolescent, he boxed, bare-fisted, with his brothers William and Charles, was supple of hand and foot, and, like his father, strong as an ox. With his hands in his pants pockets, he could kick nine feet high, leaving the hobnailed prints of his driving boots on a beam in the thrashing barn. By the age of twenty-one, he had earned a fighting reputation. He fought at dance halls, and did battle to keep the respect of his sixteen-year-old wife, Barbara Sullivan, at the late-night charivari after they were married in Blackville's

Church of the Holy Trinity in 1896. (This is the church where I was christened and in whose graveyard many of my kinfolk now sleep.) It was said that the whoops of the men on their wedding night awakened barnyards and brought working people to their windows. In the Miramichi of my grandfather's youth, rowdiness was in fashion.

The next day, with light hearts, Papa and Gram poled a white pine dugout canoe loaded down with all their worldly possessions ten miles up the river to Keenan, where Tom had inherited a farm from his aunt Sarah. Much of the farm was meadowland that had never been touched by a plowshare or scythe. This is the farm where my father was conceived and born, in sight of the river. This is the beautiful country where I was born and raised, and where my river camp is located.

It was said of Tom Curtis that he was a man's man, that he would never start a fight but would end one awfully quick. But I believe he actually liked combat and, throughout his long life, had a boyish infatuation with that dangerous amusement. As a man in his seventies he was still being called upon to act as bouncer in dance halls, and in his mid-eighties, he would challenge this grandson in a boxing match. Papa was a showperson, just as his oldest sister Marguerite had been. She moved to the United States in her early twenties and became an actress; she even performed at Carnegie Hall, in 1910. Marguerite died in Boston on July 4, 1953, at the age of eighty-nine, and her remains were shipped back to the Miramichi by train. Yes, old Broadway sleeps in a churchyard here in Blackville.

As a young man growing up on that turbulent White Rapids section of the Miramichi River, my grandfather learned how to turn handsprings on drifting logs, make a canoe out of a pine trunk, and throw a salmon spear into the reflections of a wire crew-pot, in which a pitch-wood fire illuminated the river's bottom to attract fish. He told me that he always speared his fish just in front of the back fin, which killed them instantly. Papa did this for the immediate family and for the big cousinhood around White Rapids, supplying the fish for their winter's salt barrels.

With his first cousin Joe Smith, a trapper who later perished on Holmes Lake when he broke through a covering of December ice, Papa went to pools like the Salmon Hole on the Dungarvon River, a tributary to the Miramichi, via the Renous, or perhaps to Salmon Brook on the Cains, and they would spear a truck-wagon-load of fall salmon in one night, thus supplying a logging operation with a winter's saltfish. (There's a salmon mounted on a pine slab a yard wide and two yards long hanging over the mantelpiece in my cabin. It was caught in Papa's day, and mounted by Jim Dale, a taxidermist and undertaker who had a shop in Blackville. That salmon would have weighed over forty pounds.)

I can remember the old man telling me stories of those all-night adventures, in vivid detail: the big, rugged men; the great wood-spoked truck-wagons; the able draft horses in blinders laboring under the harness as they hauled the night's catch along the old portage roads to the clink of shod hoofs, deeper into the pine woods, farther to the lumber camps, on some log-driving stream, perhaps the North Pole—a tributary to the Little Southwest Miramichi—or the North branch of the Renous, where the cooks awaited his fish for the crew.

Papa's cousin Joe was a poet, a published songwriter, and a singer of folk ballads even then. Papa said that Joe Smith could make a groan, deep in his throat, that resembled a church organ. When they were traveling on those fish wagons through the woods, they would stop for a little nip, then Joe would play the organ and Papa would sing—songs such as "Peter Emberley," which was written by John Calhoun, Papa's upriver contemporary, and "A Winter on Renous," which was written by Joe Smith himself.

The Miramichi River and its tributaries were teeming with salmon in those days, and that is a good part of why my family settled here, and, in fact, still lives here. Like the lumber trade, the river and its Atlantic salmon were a major source of our livelihood, our culture, and our spirit, just as the songs proclaim.

My father, John Curtis, was born in 1911, the youngest son of Tom and Barbara. (They raised twelve children in all.) Daddy was also by nature a river man. But my father was never a fighter; rather, he was indifferent to such foolishness, the kindest, most passive man I ever knew. In his early years, he was a farmer/woodsman. He was also a singer of country ballads and a night drifter for salmon. Then he became an angler, and later on, an outfitter and guide. And then he turned into a conservationist.

During the Great Depression of the 1930s, my father and his neighbors netted their own fall salmon. Sometimes they sold a few fish to the train men for money to buy tea, sugar, or tobacco, or maybe just enough pocket change to get into a dance. Mostly, though, they fished to fill the winter's salt barrel. Using a ten-fathom fine-twine gillnet on clear fall nights, they drifted past our farm, down around that big bend in the river below the mouth of the Cains that the sport anglers now refer to as the Golden Horseshoe. There my father and his neighbors filled their big board boats, which were difficult to pole against the currents full of salmon and grilse. They unloaded their catches on the flood meadows near our farmhouse to be divided equally among the crew, and distributed them by means of a long-shafted, home-built wheelbarrow, a tin lantern on its front, blinking along from farm to farm. The slime-covered fish sloshed around in the concaves of the wheelbarrow's box, the iron wheel crunched the sod, and the men's gum boots slipped and slid on the frosty grass as they clutched the shafts and struggled to keep the loads from tipping over.

The men always caught their salmon after the oats had been harvested, because the fall-run fish were not so fat and were considered better for salting. During those cool nights of drifting, a woman was posted on a hillside, in a place where she could see up the river for a long way. If she saw wardens approaching by canoe, she'd fire a shotgun into the air so the men would have time to get their nets, their fish, and their boats off the water before the law arrived.

But there were not many wardens in those days, and it was understood that the river people would get their winter's food supply this way come fall. Later, we filled our salt barrels with salmon legally, by means of fly casting.

When I was a child in the late '40s and early '50s, I already had an infatuation with angling. In truth, I had been fishing long before I started school. At this time, the art of angling was for me in its most primitive stages. But during those primary years, I had an unconscious love of nature, and of course, I hated the classroom. Beautiful as they were, I despised those early September mornings when I had to walk to Keenan School to be imprisoned for another long day. It was an age to be out of doors, a romantic time of year. The cool winds blew across our reaped fields, the purple crabapples dropped from the trees, and the bark of rifles could be heard in the woods back of the school. I can still hear the sound of those guns, see in their echoes the buck deer on the run.

I can smell the dampness of morning dew on the schoolhouse steps, the stale bread and jam sandwiches, the chalk and musty books enshrouded in a veil of discipline around the desk of my aunt Lillian, a no-nonsense figure who had been teaching in that classroom since my father's schooldays. (She is telling me how to line my new scribbler with a ruler, and I can smell her body odor under the mask of perfumes.) It was not easy to keep my mind on an assignment when the winds were making the big river sparkle and dance outside the classroom windows. Because, according to the adults, this was the time of year when the push was on to fill the salt barrels with deer meat and salmon.

As Aunt Lillian read the lessons, I daydreamed about being on the shore, at some eddy shaded by a pine tree. Or maybe casting from my father's old board boat, moored in front of home. In those daydreams, I could see down into the water where salmon and trout swam past me like shadows against washed gravel and the chubs hung motionlessly in the currents to dart at my baited hook. To get bait, I would have walked behind my father picking up angleworms as he plowed the garden with a slew-footed old horse that had never worn shoes, and then I would run to the river, where the scent of blossom was strongest and those big fish were jumping, always jumping. Like Daddy, I had a romantic imagination.

And even now those symbols keep me bound to a half-forgotten past, the days before I had a decent tackle, when everything river-related was bigger than real life.

I hooked and landed my first salmon on June 4, 1951. It was evening, and the sky was an unmixed blue, white cloudlets adrift, the breeze blowing the snow-white blossoms from the bird-cherry trees to sprinkle the river with confetti that floated past me as I stood waist-deep without wading boots and cast my fly hook into the boils of Papa's Rock. I was eight years old and in grade two. I had bought a split bamboo rod, reel, and line from a mail-order catalogue a month before, and had learned how to cast the tapered fly line.

On this occasion, I had stolen away to the river as country boys do when the farm chores are finally done and the outside world is so far away. I can still remember the big splash when that salmon came to the surface to take my fly, the pull from below, the upending leaps, the long down-river runs that made the line burn my fingers, the eventual exposure of the tip of its tail and dorsal fin as it tired. All of which meant that if things went according to plan and the tackle stood up, my family would be eating salmon boiled or fried at suppertime the next evening. It was a big salmon, but I don't know how much it weighed, because it was not our custom to weigh a fish. It was the experience that made that fish the size that it was, and the size it is now remembered, enhanced, no doubt, by the brushstroke of nostalgia. The excitement of catching my first salmon alone proved to be further seductive, and I spent all my free time either fly-fishing or thinking about the river. There was not much else to do in the country of my childhood.

Sometimes I shared my new tackle with a cousin, who, when a salmon was caught, made sure that it was divided between the families. Sometimes these fish were shared with a classmate. In those days, my school chums and I used to argue about which was the best sport, salmon angling or partridge hunting? For we were all passionate lovers of rod and gun and were saving our pennies toward the purchase of both. But I can never quite grasp that old day, not with the same anxiety or carefreeness. As happens through life, youthful experiences, even recollections of indifference, are eventually colored by romanticism, so that no such amusements can truly be relived with the same nuance and passion as of old. I guess it was said best by Sergei Aksarov: "Old bottles will not hold new wine, and old hearts are unfit to bear the feelings of youth."

By the late '50s, my father had built a log cabin on the riverbank in front of our farmhouse and had become a small-time outfitter. We depended more and more upon the fish as commerce, not only as food, though my father's sport fishers were never money people and some actually left camp in the night without paying for their lodging or my mother's fine meals. As a gofer around the sports, I picked up some of their ideas about angling, along with a tobacco addiction that haunts me to this day. I also got some hand-me-down equipment, including flies, hip waders, and a long-handled gaff, which was legal in those days before hook-and-release became the law. But in our family, fly-fishing for salmon was more than just a sport—salmon remained a big part of our survival, our livelihood, and our culture, our only means to fill the winter's salt cask.

I can still see the big wooden barrels that stood in our summer kitchen, the bags of coarse salt hard as rocks. I can see my grandfather, in a butcher's apron, whetting his knife, a few salmon lying on the floor's wide boards to be split down the back so that their bellies and heads could be filled with salt and layered in a barrel. I still think of salmon in terms of barrels, not schools, not pounds or inches. And certainly not being held up in a photograph. For we were told by Papa never to take a picture of a dead or dying fish, that it was sacrilegious to do this to a species so sacred to our well-being. Besides, they all looked alike to us, all filled with the same rock salt and layered in the same barrel.

Sometimes, even now, I close my eyes and try to recapture those special boyhood days. I think of that old summer kitchen with its rough board walls, the hand-hewn beams whitewashed, pots and pans hanging on nails above the giant wood-burning range with its simmering teapot and the wood-handled clothes irons that, when we went fishing in the early morning, were still warm from the night before. And the potted flowers that stood on the windowsills, a custom from my mother's side of the family. I think of Papa in his flannel shirt, his sleeves rolled up, the wide, sweat-stained suspenders, the straw hat tilted over one ear, the drooping mustache, the straight-stemmed pipe. He might have been a character out of Faulkner's Mississippi.

I can recall, with pleasure, going to Blackville with Grandfather for more salt: five miles over a dirt road to Quinn's Mercantile, rattling along in the old half-ton with a foxtail fixed to its hood ornament and windows that would not crank down. Twice, I had to grab the steering wheel to keep the truck on the road while Papa lit his pipe, coughing and puffing to fill the cab with smoke. The old man was singing "It Was I Who Killed the Swamp Robin," a song from his youth. That day, Papa was as good-natured as I had ever seen him, and, I suspect, as happy as he dared to be without bad luck following, for he was superstitious when it came to fun and laughter. Of course by that time, my grandfather was ninety years old; his voice had lost much of its power, and he was easily silenced into long periods of sleep, even as he sat upright in the truck (another reason to grab the wheel) or at home in his rocking chair, where he woke up from his fits of coughing, his eyes tearful. His Herculean strength had vanished in the ravages of time, and his thinning hair was white as cotton.

In the store with its varnished wainscoting and pressed-tin ceiling, I smelled the hampers of citrus fruit, the bulk candies, and the giant cans of tobacco that lined the shelves. There were jelly beans in a jar, from which I bought ten cents' worth.

I felt nothing but love and pity for my aged grandfather, because of course he was *not* okay; he was nearing death. He slept a bigger portion of every day, and when he died on a stormy night that winter, my brothers and I dug his grave, picking through a bed of frozen shale in the old Blackville cemetery, so he could rest in peace beside his sister, Marguerite. And I can remember thinking that nature has a beauty all of its own, even in winter—especially in winter. It has a way of erasing all unpleasant impressions from an old day of hard work and worry. My grandmother, eight years his junior, followed him to the grave eleven years later.

The rains came and new fish came up the river, salmon whose ancestors had been pursued by my forebears, who had failed to capture them. My older brother, Winston, was the fly-tier in the family; and using the old-fashioned bait hooks, off-set, with the straight eyes, he put together a combination of homemade patterns with my mother's black thread, fingernail polish, yarn, hen and duck feathers, squirrel tails, bear, dog, goat and calf hair. Some he constructed into slow-water designs with hackles that breathed and came to life, that even skipped, when retrieved properly on the desired cast and swing. Win also tied the dry flies, the bombers, and the streamers from the tails of deer and moose. And even today when I see patterns that are nearly his in catalogues or in the showcases of the big sporting goods stores, I think that maybe my brother could have invented them.

Through trial and error, my brothers, sister, and I had learned how to fish the proper angles of casts, and the speed of retrieve the fly hook required on the ninety-, seventy-five-, or forty-five-degree swing, the different strokes practiced in the pickup, the different pull and release in the false cast, the shoot—and sometimes a combination of all of the above—that a given stretch of water demanded if we were to hook and land our day's quota of salmon. There were the hit-and-move presentation, the floating drift, and the slow underwater swing, with some or no hand action. And there was the lazy forty-five-degree cast that is so commonly used today and that is taught in fly-fishing schools as a fundamental for the novice angler. But we had learned, perhaps through desperation, the more effective angles and speeds, and we knew the water and could divine where a salmon would be resting, if it was on the take, and what the fish demanded before it would strike and eventually be dragged by the gills up the hill. For we had learned to think like salmon. And each one of us brought his or her own personality to the quest, his or her own country child distinctiveness of character. There was nothing uniform or academic here, save for the rod and reel.

Later I would get my fly hooks from Everett Price, an asthmatic old man who was also a violinist. He had a small fly-tying shop in Blackville. I traded feathers, squirrel tails, and deer tails for the classic hooks that he had become famous for, had supplied to big world outfitters for a lifetime. My most productive fly pattern from Mr. Price was the Oriole, and I landed hundreds of grilse and salmon on that hook. Years later, after my mentor had passed on and I had built my own cabin on the river, I named the place Camp Oriole after that productive boyhood fly hook. And even today when I see an Oriole fly hook or hear the strains of a violin, I think of Everett Price and my early days of angling my old home stream.

My brothers, sister, and I fly-fished every evening after school, on Saturdays, and on holidays. The Miramichi is a big river where it flows past our farm, so we had to learn how to cast long and straight in all conditions—wind, rain, or sleet—if the salt barrel was going to be filled. In the fall of the year, the push was on, and sometimes, when the end of the season was drawing near and the cask still half empty, my brothers and I jigged school. I can remember one morning after the school bus had gone, Win and I stole away to the river, where we caught eight salmon before noon. When, at dinnertime, we carried these fish up the hill and into the old summer kitchen and laid them on the floor, my grandfather was happy and set out to fillet them for the barrel. But my mother was furious because we had not got on the bus. She told us that she did not want to see her children grow up in ignorance, and that because we were poor, we'd have to work harder to break new ground. My mother had grown up in the country, but she was a good reader and didn't preach the old country ways.

I started my career as a river guide in the summer of '59. Hughie Pnaff, a man from Vermont, was staying at my father's camp and had, after just one day, become a close friend to the family, so he was getting a reduced rate. In the evening, he and my father stood beside Mother's piano, drank his Scotch whisky, and sang the old country songs of Hank Williams—"I'm a rolling stone, all alone and lost." The next morning, he asked me if I knew the river, and where could we go to find him a salmon?

"I don't know," I told him. "Let's have a go at Papa's Rock and we'll see what happens."

He waded out to his waist and started casting into the boils the big rock made near center stream. I saw a splash and heard him shout, "Hey, lad, I got one on!"

He hooked three grilse that morning before ten a.m. and was a happy camper. Of course, when it came to that stretch of water, I knew the music it would make, if fished properly from top to bottom, and was not just repeating instructions I'd learned by rote; I'd learned by trial and error, by a whole childhood on the river. I guided the man for three falls, even though I was underage and had no guide's license. Each year, along with my wages of five dollars a day, he tipped me with a carton of Camel cigarettes. By the fourth fall he returned, I had moved on to the city to look for a winter's work.

Still, over the next fifty years, I guided a good part of every angling season. I have worked for all the major outfitters along the Miramichi, and some not so major. You learn a lot about a river that way—standing in the water, instructing the fishers to do what comes natural to those of us who grew up here. It's funny how brain surgeons or rocket scientists can hang themselves if you put a fishing rod in their hands.

One fall, a woman from the Doctor's Island Fishing Lodge taught me how to barbecue a salmon over hardwood coals, roasting it flesh side down for twenty minutes, with only salt and pepper added. We did this every day for two weeks, leaving the lodge without a lunch, depending only upon my guiding advice and her casting arm to provide us with our midday meal. This was back in the day when Marilyn Monroe was said to be fishing here, and during those fall cookouts, I kept an eye on passing canoes, in hopes of getting a glimpse of her. But I never saw her, nor did anyone I talked to along the river. Even today, when I have a family barbecue at Camp Oriole, I cook my salmon in that way. It has become my signature dish. The scent of salmon roasting and the melancholy of an old country song still reflect images first of my father with his Serenade guitar, and then of Marilyn Monroe, not on the river for sure, but in the movies.

Not all of my guests were that much fun to be around. At Wade's Fishing Lodge, an undertaker from New York was a heavy boozer and threatened to bury me that evening if we didn't have a fish in the boat by five o'clock. Our party of six anglers and their guides were lunching at midday on the shore at the Oxbow Pool on the Cains. When the senior guide, Jack Brophy, overheard these words, he said to the New Yorker, for all to hear, "We bury undertakers in this river too! Now, did you come here to fish or to fight?"

"No, to fish!" he said with astonishment. "I came to fish!"

Old Man Brophy calmed down after that, and I had no more trouble with the undertaker. Still, understanding how passionate he was about catching a salmon, I was feeling a kind of pressure I had not previously experienced, not even in the hungry days of fishing for the supper table. For when you are a guide, you want to do your job well, to develop a reputation that will attract future clients. So at four-thirty, I asked him if I could try his rod. We did get a fish that afternoon, and my life was spared. Still, the undertaker left disgruntled, and without leaving a tip. It was great to see his backside.

At Black Rapids Lodge, while trying to scoop an angler's salmon—his first one in a week of casting—I fell into the river right over my head, and when my waders filled with water, I had to be helped to shore, coughing. "No need to drown yourself," my guest told me, laughing. "It's only a fish. I'm here mostly for the conversation anyway."

At the Miramichi Inn on the Little Southwest, I had a wading angler drift away in the heavy currents of the Foran Rapids. He had not heard what I told him above the roar of the water and had gone out too far. He would have drowned had I not been able to run down the shore, wade out and grasp his arm, and drag him onto the gravel beach. He was as lifeless as a rag and overtired from battling the intake of water.

I have saved at least two men from drowning over the years. And there was one I could not save. On the 26th of April 1971, Dr. Niles Perkins of Bowdoinham, Maine, went into the water when his boat overturned in the big river, which was just two degrees above freezing. With heavy clothes on, you can't swim, and he went under before any of us guides could get to him. There are no bravery medals or accolades for river guides, not like the police, not like the search-and-rescue units, not like the military. For a guide, it's all in a day's work, calamity, storms, and high water notwithstanding. There is no union protection against abusive clients or outfitters who seek guarantees, no curfews on working hours, no liability rules when it comes to river or weather hazards. And there is that old river wisdom: *When you are on the water with a guest, everything that can go wrong will go wrong.*

However, most of my professional river experiences were memorable and without calamity. My own river camp was built in 1974 on a section of the old home property I inherited from my father and mother. Daddy and I used white pine logs, the corners notched into dovetails. It is a good, solid cabin with a stone fireplace. In back of the camp yard is a swampy meadow, with bog holes and hillocks and tall poplar trees, where the leaves dance from the river winds and from which the musical phrases of birds, toads, and frogs color the air. Out front, on breezy days, the broad, slow-moving river shimmers like a sheet of steel under the sun's reflections. In the evenings, perhaps after a shower that has turned the weather-beaten farm buildings from gray to black—the most beautiful time of day—the shoreline trees reflect into the mirror-smooth water. And I can see the salmon that school past from my seat on the veranda.

Through the years, when I was not working as a guide, I fished with my sons, Jeff, Jason, and Steven. They were just small boys in the '70s, but on the river, I could see in them a part of my early self, my father, and my grandfather. In mid-June, when the schools were closed for the summer, we would leave our modern home in the estuary and move to the cabin, where we stayed until September. This was our little provincial universe, with its own center of gravity, and we didn't want to leave it. We fished those old home waters for weeks running, and sometimes we took three-day excursions to tributaries such as the North Pole stream, the Dungarvon, or the Cains, tenting along the shores of those wonderful salmon rivers, cooking hot dogs and brewing tea on open campfires. Sometimes we left the cabin and went for a hike to Morse Brook, where we fished Aunt Edith's Hole or the big beaver dams up in back of our old property lines. (My great-aunt Edith had been a lover of trout angling during the '50s when she was home from Duluth on summer vacations, and went there often.) We got trout for the breakfast frying pan. The logging roads in back of the camp, where I had lumbered and hunted deer with my father as a boy, though overgrown, were still easy to follow, and sometimes we chanted our way along, following the converging wheel ruts, the lyrics of an old country song. And having the boys along on these little expeditions, having them experience the same things that I had as a youngster, meant all the world to me.

My then wife, the late Janet Manderville, must have been a saint to tolerate so much frivolous river talk—the comparing of tackle, the technique used on such and such a water, the river's geography and character in general. For these river things monopolized the conversations. Sometimes she came with us on canoe runs down the Cains or Renous, when we paddled through the long days and made camp on the shore; there we fought flies, with the smoke of a campfire stinging our eyes. Some days we battled an upriver wind for hours on end before we got to our destination. As time went on, Janet's trips with the family became more and more seldom, and she appeared to be indifferent to the raggedness of the terrain and the elements. But on those outings, my sons hooked and landed their first salmon by the ages of eight. And of course, they cranked in many sea-run brook trout. Thus we reenacted the old tradition. And our love for the river, and each other, was like an addiction that we had no desire to overcome.

Those were wonderful days when my boys were small and my mother and father were still well and active and came to our cabin for birthday parties and fondues. We had big celebrations on the year's closing day. We compared our river diaries to see who had outfished whom. Sometimes at those parties I showed a film of Lee Wulff, fly-fishing with light tackle on Newfoundland's Portland Creek in the 1940s. (In later years Lee became a friend, and was my sponsor when I joined the Outdoor Writers Association of America.) Or maybe a film that featured Ted Williams, formerly of the Boston Red Sox, who lived near our cabin in those days and whom I had fished with many times. Sometimes it was a kitchen party with fiddling, step-dancing, and singing. Even today the songs of John Denver carry in their melodies images from closing day.

Back then, during my own summer holidays, I would sit on the veranda by a card table and write articles for those wildlife magazines you see in tobacco shops. (On their covers, the mule deer have exaggerated antlers and the fish are so much bigger and wilder than anything in real life.) It was before the age of computers, and I was using an old iron typewriter with letters that would not punch out clearly and a cylinder that jammed the paper.

Sometimes in the heat of the afternoon I took a break from my work and went to the river where the children were swimming. And I would sit in the coolness of the tall shore grass, soon to fall under my father's scythe, and observe the scene, as a kind of research. This was where, in Papa's day, the big logjams crowded the river from shore to shore, and the young men ran on them in shows of bravado—to drop through meant a certain death. This was where our team of horses broke through the ice while pulling bobsleds loaded with two cords of maple stove wood, my grandfather shouting, "We gotta throw the wood off, before we lose sleds and all!" The horses and crew survived the incident unharmed, but it was touch and go for a while. This was where, at twilight one August evening, I watched a black bear grab a salmon from the shallows and run with it into the trees. The fish had gone into the mouth of Mackenzie Brook, where the water was colder but very shallow. And I can still see the long-abandoned farmhouse, now screened by a stand of trees.

Even now, especially now, these images offer a kind of prose that is beyond words. We the river people are so much a part of the landscape, the riverscape, which we inhabit and which controls our moods and dreams. The river lands have the power to hold us on course. It might be through something as subtle as a crow's fleeting shadow across a country lane, a mission bell remote on the breeze, or a setting sun that shines through a broken cloud to make golden wheel-spokes in the sky. Indeed, there is no language to describe the heart-shared feelings conveyed by such images to people who are wrong to the sounds and senses, and so can never hear or see them. This is a language only for those who have witnessed these experiences, shared the passion and the river spirit.

Of course, things have changed since the days of fly-fishing for the salt barrel. Times got better, so there is no desperation, no pressure to bring home a fish for the supper table. Angling for Atlantic salmon became instead a chance to practice something entrenched in our bloodstreams for generations. Hook-and-release laws came into effect, so we no longer dragged fish of any size up the hill. The equipment also changed, to ultramodern, lightweight rods that throw a fly hook farther than I ever dreamed of doing as a young man. Lines, leaders, and reels modernized. And of course, it's a different river today, too, one with fewer fish. This can make life difficult for my son Jason, a professional river guide, as he tries to please a client who has booked his or her fishing days months in advance. The quality of the angling is hard to predict, even for long-standing river people. But this is still a beautiful river, its waters clear and cold, with an excellent sea-run trout population and a superb salmon fishery that helps even now to drive the river's economy.

On special outings, like Father's Day or perhaps a family birthday, we celebrate at the river camp. My grandsons, Samuel and Joshua, come with their father and uncles. The boys are in their first years of elementary school, but already they too are experienced river people and are fitted out with modern equipment, including life jackets, sunscreen, and other protective devices that as a boy I never would have thought of owning. When we are fishing together, I look at them, each making the long cast, experimenting with the angles, practicing the retrieve, the drift, sometimes even a mend—though I never believed in mending, not for this fish. Rather, I preach the straight cast, with a swing, like the pendulum of a grandfather clock. Still, watching them, I can see a part of myself.

In the past few years, I have turned down many would-be clients. While I need the money, and indeed the camaraderie of new acquaintances, I find the mental and physical strain is too taxing on my time-worn body and soul. Having suffered one heart attack, I no longer have the stamina to work as a river guide, to travel the long days, in and out of the water, up and down the steep inclines to and from the cabins, poling loaded canoes against the currents. I can now only dream of getting to the places where I used to angle with success. But the aches and pains in my bones keep the presence of the river flowing around me, even as I write this.

Nowadays I stay in camp, with its big window fronting the river, and observe the scenery, and any activity that may be happening in the old home waters. I watch the out-of-country anglers standing in waist-deep water, casting, casting, their faces glowing against the sun's brilliance. I feel the mystery of their expectations, their anticipation of the moment that has brought them here—the splash, the big pull, the salmon's long run that will give them a youthful thrill.

In my night dreams, or the insomnia between dreams, I hear the anglers' bark, crisp and clear above the din of water. I see the bending rods, the yellow casting lines that cut the water like a twine through vodka. And I jump to my feet in a panic, looking to give a hand in landing the fish, only to find that I am in my cabin, alone.

Stealhead Joe

BY IAN FRAZIER

*A version of this essay was previously
published in* Outside *magazine.*

THE POLICE REPORT listed the name of the deceased as
Joseph Adam Randolph and his age as forty-eight. It did
not mention the name he had given himself: Stealhead Joe.
The address on his driver's license led police to his former
residence in Sisters, Oregon, where the landlord said that
Randolph had moved out over a year ago and had worked
as a fishing guide. In fact, Randolph was one of the most
skilled guides on the nearby Deschutes River, and certainly
the most colorful—even unforgettable—in the minds of
anglers who had fished with him.

He had specialized in catching sea-run fish called steelhead, and was so devoted to the sport that he had a large
steelhead fly with two drops of blood at the hook point tat-
tooed on the inside of his right forearm. The misspelling of

his self-bestowed moniker was intentional. If he didn't actually steal fish, he came close, and he wanted people to hear echoes of the trickster and the outlaw in his name.

I spent six days fishing with Stealhead Joe in early September of 2012, two months before he died. I planned to write a profile of him for a magazine and had been trying for a year to set up a trip. Most guides' reputations stay within their local area, but Joe's had extended even to where I live, in New Jersey.

Somehow, though, I could never get him on the phone. Once, finding myself in Portland with a couple of days free, I drove down to Sisters in the hope of booking a last-minute trip, but when I asked for him at the Fly Fishers Place, the shop where he worked, I was told, in essence, "Take a number!" Staffers laughed and showed me his completely filled-out guiding schedule on a calendar on an office door, Joe himself being unreachable "on the river" for the next x days.

The timing sorted itself out eventually. Joe and I spoke, we made arrangements to fish together, and I met him in Maupin, a small town on the Deschutes about ninety miles from Sisters. Joe had moved to Maupin for personal and professional reasons since I'd first looked for him in Sisters. On the day we met, a Sunday, I called Joe at nine in the morning to say I was in town. He said he was in the middle of folding his laundry but would stop by my motel when he was done. I sat on a divider in the motel parking lot and waited. His vehicle could be identified from far off. It was a red 1995 Chevy Tahoe with a type of fly rod called a spey extending from a holder on the hood to another holder on the roof, like a long, swept-back antenna.

I have seen a few beat-up fishing vehicles, and even owned one or two of them myself. This SUV was a beaut, and I chuckled in appreciation as Joe got out, introduced himself, and showed me its details. The Tahoe's color was a dusty western red, like a red shirt that gets brighter as you slap dust off of it. (To maintain that look, he deliberately did not wash his vehicle, a girlfriend of Joe's would later tell me.) The grille had been broken multiple times by deer Joe had hit while speeding down country roads in predawn darkness in order to be on the water before everybody else, or while returning in the night after other anglers had gone home. He had glued it back together with epoxy, and there was still deer hair in the mends.

Hanging from the inside rearview mirror was a large red-and-white plastic fishing bobber on a loop of monofilament line, and on the dash and in the cup holders were coiled-up tungsten-core leaders, steelhead flies, needle-nose pliers— "numerous items consistent with camping and fishing," as the police report would later put it. While Joe and I were admiring his truck, I didn't guess I was looking at the means he would use to take his life. He died in the driver's seat, which he pushed back into its full reclining position for the occasion. The report gave the cause of death as asphyxiation from carbon-monoxide poisoning.

Something momentous always seems about to happen in canyon towns like Maupin, where the ready supply of gravity suggests velocity and disaster. Above the town, to the east and west, the high desert of central Oregon spreads its dusty brown wheat fields toward several horizons. Below the town, in a canyon that is wide in some places and narrow in others, 4,500 cubic feet per second of jade-colored river go rushing by.

Four-hundred-some people live in Maupin in the winter; several thousand might occupy it on any weekend from June through Labor Day. People come to whitewater raft, mainly, and to fish. Guys plank on bars in the wee hours, tequila shots are drunk from women's navels, etc. Sometimes daredevils pencil-dive from Maupin's one highway bridge; the distance between the Gothic-style concrete railing and the river is ninety-eight feet. They spread their arms and legs in the instant after impact so as not to hit the bottom too hard.

Maupin, an ordinary small western town to most appearances, actually deals in the extraordinary. What it offers is transcendence; people can experience huge, rare thrills around here. Fishing for steelhead is one of them.

Steelhead are rainbow trout that begin life in freshwater rivers, swim down to the ocean, stay there for years, and come back up their native rivers to spawn, sometimes more than once. They grow much bigger than rainbows that never leave fresh water, and they fight harder, and they shine a brighter silver—hence their name.

To get to the Deschutes from the ocean, the steelhead must first swim up the Columbia River and through the fish ladders at the Bonneville and Dalles dams, massive power-generating stations that (I believe) add a zap of voltage to whatever the fish do thereafter. Some are hatchery fish, some aren't, but all have the size, ferocity, and wildness associated with the ocean. "Fishing for steelhead is hunting big game," says John Hazel, the senior of all the Deschutes River guides and co-owner of the Deschutes Angler, a fly shop in Maupin.

Steelhead are elusive, selective, sometimes not numerous, and largely seasonal. They seem to prefer the hardest-to-reach parts of this fast, rock-cluttered, slippery, rapid-filled, generally unhelpful river. On the banks, you must watch for rattlesnakes. Fishing from a boat is not allowed. You wade deeper than you want, and then you cast, over and over. You catch mostly nothing.

Casting for steelhead is like calling God on the telephone; it rings and rings and rings, hundreds of rings, a thousand rings, and you listen to each ring as if an answer might come at any moment, but no answer comes, and no answer comes, and then on the 1,001st ring, or the 1,047th ring, God loses his patience and picks up the phone and yells, "WHAT THE HELL ARE YOU CALLING ME FOR?" in a voice the size of the canyon. You would fall to your knees if you weren't chest-deep in water and afraid that the rocketing, leaping creature you have somehow tied into will get away.

Joe's other nicknames (neither of which he gave himself) were Melanoma Joe and Nymphing Joe. The second referred to his skill at fishing for steelhead with aquatic insect imitations called nymphs. This method uses a bobber or other floating strike indicator and a nymph at a fixed distance below it in the water. Purists don't approve of fishing this way; they say it's too easy and not much different from dangling a worm in front of the fish's nose.

For himself, Joe believed in the old-time method of casting downstream and letting the fly swing across the current in classical, purist style. But he also taught himself to nymph, and taught others, and a lot of Joe's clients caught a lot of fish by this method. In one of Joe's obituaries, Mark Few—Joe's most prized and illustrious client, the coach of the highly ranked men's basketball team at Gonzaga University, a man whom Joe called, simply, "Coach," who liked to catch a lot of fish, and who therefore fished with nymphs—praised Joe's "open-mindedness" as a guide.

The nickname Melanoma Joe came from Joe's habit of fishing in board shorts and wading boots and nothing else. Most guides long-sleeve themselves, and lotion and hat and maybe glove themselves, and some even wrap a scarf around their heads and necks and faces like mujahideen. Joe let the desert sun burn him reddish brown. Board shorts, T-shirt, sunglasses, baseball cap, flip-flops—that was his attire when we met. He grew up mostly in California, and still looked Californian.

He smoked three packs of Marlboros a day.

For a guy as lost as Joe must have been, he gave off a powerful fatherly vibe. Even I was affected by it, though he was thirteen years my junior. An hour after we met, we waded out into the middle of the Deschutes in a long, straight stretch above town. The wading freaked me out, and I was frankly holding on to Joe. He was six-five, broad shouldered,

with a slim, long-waisted swimmer's body. I wore chest waders, and Joe had put on his waders, too, in deference to the
colder water. I held tightly to his wader belt. Close up, I
smelled the Marlboro smell. When I was a boy, many adults,
and almost all adult places and pastimes, smelled of cigarettes. Joe had the same tobacco-smoke aroma I remembered
from dads of fifty years ago. I relaxed slightly; I might have
been ten years old. Joe held my hand.

That day we were in the river not primarily to catch
fish but to teach me how to cast the spey rod. I had been
dreading the instruction. Lessons on how to do any athletic
activity fail totally with me. Golf-coach reprimands like
"You're not opening up your hips on the follow-through" fall
on my ears as purest gibberish, talking in tongues, like the
lost language of a tribe of Israel that has been found again
at Pebble Beach—where Joe was once a golf pro, by the way,
as he told me in passing. The only athletic enterprises he
had never tried, he said, were boxing and wrestling. Now he
demonstrated to me the proper spey-casting method. Flour-
ishing the rod through positions one, two, three, and four,
he sent the line flying like a perfect tee shot down fairway
one. From where we were standing, above our waists in
water, it went ninety feet, dead straight. You could catch any
fish in the river with that cast.

Regular fly casting uses the weight of the line and the
resistance of the air to bend the rod, or "load" it, so that
a flick of the wrist and arm can release the tension and
shoot the line forward. Spey casting, an antique Scottish

technique from the heyday of waterpower, uses a longer rod, two hands, and the line's resistance on the surface of the river to provide the energy. You lay the line on the water beside you, bring the rod up, sweep it back over the line against the surface tension, and punch it forward with an in-out motion of your top and bottom hands. The spey cast is actually a kind of water-powered spring. It throws line farther and better than regular fly casting does, and because it involves no backcast, it is advantageous in closed-in places like the canyons of the Deschutes.

If Joe showed any signs of depression in the first days we fished together, I did not notice them. Walking along the railroad tracks beside the river on our way to a good place to fish, he seemed happy, even blithe. As we passed the carcass of a run-over deer with the white of buzzard droppings splattered all around, he said, "I've been fly-fishing since I was eight years old. Bird hunting, too. My grandfather sent me a fly rod and a 12-gauge shotgun for my eighth birthday, because he fished and hunted and wanted me to be like him. He was a Cajun from south Louisiana. His last name was Cherami. That was my mom's family, and my dad's family was also from the South, but they were more, like, aristocrats. My last name, Randolph, is an old Virginia name, and I'm actually a direct descendant of Thomas Jefferson. My dad's father is buried at Monticello."

We went down the riprap beside the tracks and held back the pricker bushes for each other. They were heavy with black raspberries; the smell in the cooler air by the water was like someone making jam. Joe stopped to look at the Deschutes before wading in. "This is the greatest river in America," he said. "It's the only one I know of that's both a great steelhead river and a blue-ribbon trout stream. The way I came to it was, I was married to Florence Belmondo. Do you know who Jean-Paul Belmondo is? Famous French movie actor? You do? Cool! A lot of people never heard of him. Anyway, Florence is his daughter. She's an amazing person, very sort of withdrawn in a group, but warm and up for anything—like, she has no fear—and knockout beautiful on top of that. We met on a blind date in Carmel, California, and were together from then on. Flo and I got married in 2003, and we did stuff like stay at Belmondo's house in Paris and his compound in Antigua."

I looked at Joe, both to make sure he was being serious and to reexamine his face. I observed that he looked a bit like Belmondo himself—the same close-set, soulful eyes, big ears, and wry, down-turned mouth.

Florence skis, Joe was a snowboarder. They began to visit central Oregon for the snow at Mount Bachelor, Joe discovered the Deschutes, Florence got him a guided trip on the river as a present, he fell in love with the river, they moved to Sisters, and she bought them a big house in town in 2005. "After I learned the river and started my own guiding, I think that was what created problems between Florence and me," Joe said.

"Being a kept man sounds great, but it's really not. To be honest, there were other problems, too. So finally we divorced. That was in '08. We tried to get back together once or twice, but it didn't work out. Well, anyway—man, it was awesome being married to her. I'll always be grateful to her, because she's the reason I came here and found this river. And I have no desire to fish anywhere else but on the Deschutes for the rest of my life."

The railroad tracks we were walking on belong to the Burlington Northern Santa Fe Railway. During the day, the trains sound their horns and rattle Maupin's stop signs and bounce echoes around the canyon. At night they are quieter; if trains can be said to tiptoe, these do. The rhythmic sound of their wheels rises, fills your ears, and fades; the silence after it's gone refills with the sound of the river. We were out in the night in Maupin a lot because first light and last light are good times to catch steelhead. It seems to me now that I spent as much time with Joe in the dark as I did in the light.

On my second night, he and I went to a fish hatchery downstream from town. We parked, zigzagged down a slope, passed dark buildings, crossed a lawn, and wrong-footed our way along the tracks, on whose curving rails the moon had laid a dull shine. After about a mile, we plunged through some alders and into the river and stood in the water for a long time waiting for dawn to start. This all felt a bit spooky and furtive to me.

My instinct, I later learned, was right. I had a fishing license, and Joe had licenses both to fish and to guide. He did not, however, possess a valid permit to be a fishing guide on the Deschutes. Two months earlier, he had left the Fly

Fisher's Place in Sisters (actually, he had been fired), and thus he had lost the guiding permit that the shop provided him. His attempt to jury-rig one from a rafting guide's permit loaned to him by an outfitter in Maupin was not enough, because it allowed him to guide rafters but not anglers. Joe was breaking the law, in other words, and the consequences could be a fine of up to $2,500, a possible prison term, and the forfeit of his guiding license—no small risk to run.

On some evenings, after fishing, Joe and I went to Maupin's bars. They were packed with a young crowd that included many rafting guides, and everybody seemed to know Joe. He sat drinking beers and watching two or more baseball games on the bar TVs while young guys came up to him, often asking for advice—"She's kissed me twice, Joe, and I mean, *she* kissed *me*. But I haven't even brought up anything about sex." Joe: "Hell, tee her up, man, and ask questions later!" At the end of the night a barmaid announced last call, and Joe told her, "I'll have another beer, and a cot."

When Tiger Woods fished the Deschutes some years ago (with John Hazel, not with Joe), he did not pick up the spey cast right away, so I guess it's no surprise that I didn't either. I simply couldn't get the message, and I told Joe I wanted to go back to the fly rod. Not possible, he said. He had no fly rod; and, at his insistence, I had not brought mine. He was a patient and remorseless coach, smoking and commenting on each attempt as I tried over and over. "You fucked up, Bud. Your rod tip was almost in the water on that last one. Keep the tip high." A failed spey cast is a shambles, like the collapse of a circus tent, with pole and line in chaos and disgrace everywhere.

But he wouldn't give up. I worried that it might be painful for him to watch something he did so beautifully being done so wrong, but now I think his depression gave him a sort of immunity. The tedium of watching me may have been nothing compared with what he was feeling inside. And when occasionally I did get it, his enthusiasm was gigantic: "That's it! *Money!*" he would holler as the line sailed out.

So I'm in my motel cabin the night before our three-day float trip, and I can't sleep. I keep practicing the motions of the cast—one, two, three, four—like the present-arms drill in a commercial for the Marine Corps on tv. I practice the cast when I'm pacing around the motel-cabin floor and when I'm lying on my back in the bed. Joe has told me that the first pool we will fish is the best pool on the entire lower river.

If I don't catch a fish there, I figure, my chances for success will go way down. He has shown me how to cast from the right side of the river and from the left; you turn the motion around, like batting from opposite sides of the plate. He has said we will fish this first pool from the right side, so I practice that cast only. I keep remembering that I have never caught a steelhead. I do not sleep a wink.

He has told me to come to his house at 3:45 a.m. The early start is essential, he has assured me, because another guide is likely to be in the pool before us if we're late. At 3:15 I put on my gear and drive to his house. All his windows are dark. The moon is up, and I wait in the shadow of Joe's trailered drift boat. No sign of activity in the house. At the tick of 3:45, I step noisily onto the front porch in my studded wading shoes and rap on the door. Through the window I can see only darkness and the corner of a white laundry basket in a patch of moonlight. I call Joe's name. A pause. Then, from somewhere inside: "Th'damn alarm didn't go off!"

He comes out, rumpled and sleepy, and puts on his waders, which were hanging on the porch rail. We get in the Tahoe and take off, stopping on the way to pick up some coffee and pastries from the free breakfast spread at a motel considerably more expensive than my own. Joe assures me this is okay; no one is around to disagree.

We rattle for half an hour down a county road beside the river, leaving dust behind, and then pull into a location he asks me not to disclose. He backs the drift boat down to the river and launches it and we get in. At the second or third scrape of the oars against the boat's aluminum sides, headlamps light up at a place not far from the boat launch. Guys are camped there so as to get to this pool at first light, and we have beaten them to it, Joe says with satisfaction. We go a short distance downstream and stop under the branches of trees on the right-hand bank.

The moon is not high enough to reach into the canyon, so the water is completely dark. We wait, not talking. I unwrap and eat the Heartland Bakery cinnamon Danish from the more expensive motel's breakfast spread and crumple the wrapper and put it in the top of my waders and rinse my fingers in the river. The sky lightens and the water becomes a pewter color. Faintly, its ripples and current patterns can now be seen. Joe puts out his cigarette and applies Chap-Stick to his lips. We slide from the boat into the river.

My fear of wading has receded, thanks partly to my new wading staff. We go halfway across the pool. Joe tells me where to put the fly—a pattern called the Green Butt Skunk—and I begin to cast. Suddenly, I'm casting well and throwing line far across the river. Joe exclaims in astonishment and yells, "Money! Goddamn! You're throwing line as good as Abe Streep!" (He is referring to an editor of *Outside* magazine, a fine athlete who fished with him the year before.) I am elated and try not to think about how I am managing to cast this well. I fish the fly across and downstream as the line swings in the current. I strip in the line, take a step downstream, and cast again.

Cast, step, cast again; I work my way down the pool, Joe next to me. We pause as a train goes by, hauling a collection of graffiti on the sides of its white boxcars. I notice a purple, bulbous scrawl that reminds me of something. Joe tells me to cast toward a pile of white driftwood on the bank. I send fifty or sixty feet of line straight at it, lay the fly beside it, swing the fly across. The light is now high enough that the ripples and the lanes of current are distinct. At the end of the swing, a swift, curved disturbance appears in the pewter surface of the river, and the line pulls powerfully tight.

Joe's father, William Randolph, was a navy pilot who flew many missions in Vietnam and could be gone for months at a time. Brenda, Joe's mother, stayed home with Joe (called

Joey), his older sister, Kay, and his younger sister, Fran. The family spent much of the kids' childhood at Naval Air Station Lemoore, south of Fresno, California, where Joe often rode his bicycle down to the Kings River to fish.

Sometimes he hunted for ducks with family friends. Later he even had a scabbard on his bicycle in which he could carry his shotgun. His friends had shotguns, too, and sometimes they would stand about a hundred yards apart in a field and shoot at each other with the lighter sizes of birdshot. The pellets did not penetrate but "stung like crazy" when they hit. Once, when Joe was speeding along on his bicycle without a helmet, he came out from behind a Dumpster and a passing garbage truck ran into him and knocked him unconscious. There was not much male supervision on the base with the dads away at war.

Joe's mother had problems with depression, which the kids did not understand until they were in their twenties. Once or twice they went to stay with relatives while she was hospitalized. When Joe was in grade school, she and his father divorced. Joe's main emotional problem, as Kay remembers, was getting angry, often at himself for personal frustrations. As a boy, he played tennis and traveled to tournaments and earned a national junior-level ranking. Being tall, he had a big serve, but his inability to avoid blowups on the court ruled out tennis for him. Other sports he excelled in were basketball, baseball, track, and volleyball.

He went to high school in Fresno but did not graduate, although he did get his GED. To acquire a useful trade, in the late 1980s he attended a school in the Midwest, where he learned to be a baker; then he decided that was not for him and returned to California. He was kicked off the basketball team at Monterey Peninsula College for skipping practice to fish. Various injuries—elbow, knee, a severe fracture of the left ankle—interfered with his promising college baseball career. He once watched a doctor chip a bone spur off his knee with a chisel and did not pass out.

In his thirties, in Monterey, he tried to qualify for the semipro beach-volleyball circuit and took steroids to improve his game. The drugs caused him to feel invincible and aggressive and righteously angry, and added a foot to his vertical leap, but he did not make the roster. While playing volleyball he met a woman named Tricia, and they married. The couple had two children—Hank, born in 1995, and Maddi, born in 1997. He and Tricia separated in about 2000 and later divorced.

Now the sun had risen over the canyon, and Joe was navigating us through rapids whose splashes wet my notebook as I recorded the details of my first steelhead—a six-pound hatchery fish from far upstream, according to the identification made by Joe on the basis of the fish's clipped maxillary fin (a tiny fin by the mouth).

"The tug is the drug," steelheaders say, describing that first strike and the fight that follows. This was true, as I could now affirm. The afterglow was great, too. I looked up at the canyon walls rising like hallelujah arms, their brown grasses crossed by eagle shadows, and at the green patches where

small springs came up, and the herd of bighorn sheep starting mini rockslides behind their back hooves, and the hatch
of tiny crane flies like dust motes in the sunlight.

Happiness! The pressure was off. I had caught the fish,
defeated the possible jinx, the article would now work
out. In this mood, I could have fallen out of the boat and
drowned and not minded, or not minded much. The morning had become hot, and Joe asked if I wanted some water.
He opened the cooler. Inside I saw a few bottles of spring
water and a thirty-pack of Keystone beer in cans. Joe's assis-
tant for the trip, a young man named J. T. Barnes, went by
in a yellow raft loaded with gear, and Joe waved. He said J.T.
would set up our evening camp downstream.

Every fishing trip reconstructs a cosmogony, a world of
angling defeats and victories, heroes and fools. Joe told me
about a guy he fished with once who hooked a bat, and the
guy laughed as the bat flew here and there at the end of his
line, and then it flew directly at the guy's head and wrapped
the line around the guy's neck and was in his face flapping
and hissing and the guy fell on the ground screaming for Joe
to get the bat off him and Joe couldn't do a thing, he was
laughing so hard.

"Do your clients ever hook you?" I asked.

"Oh, hell yes, all the time. Once I was standing on the bank
and this guy was in the river fly casting, and he wrapped his
backcast around my neck, and I yelled at him, and what does
the guy do but yank harder! Almost strangled me. I'll never
forget that fucking guy. We laughed about it later in camp."

The next pool we fished happened to be on the left side. I had not practiced the left-side cast during my insomniac night. Now when I tried it I could not do it at all. The pool after that was on the right, but my flailing on the left had caused me to forget how to cast from the right. Again the circus-tent collapse, again chaos and disgrace. My euphoria wore off, to be replaced by symptoms of withdrawal.

I liked that Joe always called me "Bud." It must have been his standard form of address for guys he was guiding. The word carried overtones of affection, familiarity, respect. He got a chance to use it a lot while trying to help me regain my cast, because I soon fell into a dire slump, flop sweat bursting on my forehead, all physical coordination gone.

"Bud, you want to turn your entire upper body toward the opposite bank as you sweep that line ... You're trying to do it all with your arms, Bud ... Watch that line, Bud, you're coming forward with it just a half second too late." I was ready to flip out, lose my temper, hurl the rod into the trees. Joe was all calmness, gesturing with the cigarette between two fingers of his right hand. "Try it again, Bud, you almost had it that time."

By mid-afternoon Joe had started in on the thirty-pack of Keystone, but he took his time with it and showed no effects. Our camp that night was at a wide, flat place that had been an airfield. J.T. served shrimp appetizers and steak. Joe and I sat in camp chairs while he drank Keystone and told more stories—about his Cajun grandfather who used to drink and pass out on fishing excursions, and Joe had to rouse him so he wouldn't trail his leg in the gator-infested waters; about a stripper he had a wild affair with, and how they happened to break up; about playing basketball at night on inner-city courts in Fresno where you put quarters in a meter to keep the playground lights on. At full dark, I went into my tent and looked through the mesh at the satellites going by. Joe stayed up and drank Keystone and watched sports on his iPhone.

I was back in the river and mangling my cast again the next morning while Joe and J.T. loaded the raft. Out of my hearing (as I learned afterward from J.T.), their conversation turned to J.T.'s father, who had died when J.T. was fifteen. Joe asked J.T. a lot of questions about how the death had affected him.

J.T. misunderstood Joe's instructions and set up our next camp at the wrong place, a narrow ledge at the foot of a sagebrush-covered slope. Joe was angry but didn't yell at him. During dinner that evening, J.T. told us the story of his recent skateboarding injury, when he dislocated his right elbow and snapped all the tendons so the bones of his forearm and hand were hanging only by the skin. Joe watched a football game and talked about Robert Griffin III, who was destined to be one of the greatest quarterbacks of all time, in Joe's opinion. As I went to bed I could still hear his iPhone's signifying noises.

At a very late hour, I awoke to total quiet and the sound of the river. The moon was pressing black shadows against the side of my tent. I got out of my sleeping bag and unzipped the tent flap and walked a distance away, for the usual middle-of-the-night purpose. When I turned to go back, I saw a figure standing in the moonlight by the camp. It was just standing there in the sagebrush and looking at me.

At first I could not distinguish the face, but as I got closer I saw that it was Joe. At least it ought to be, because he was the most likely possibility; but the figure just stood in silence, half shadowed by sagebrush bushes up to the waist. I blinked to get the sleep out of my eyes. As I got closer, I saw it had to be Joe, unquestionably. Still no sound, no sign of recognition. I came closer still. Then Joe smiled and said, "You too, Bud?" in a companionable tone. I felt a certain relief, even gratitude, at his ability to be wry about this odd moonlight encounter between two older guys getting up in the night. Now, looking back, I believe that more was going on. I believe that what I saw was a ghost—an actual person who also happened to be a ghost, or who was contemplating being one.

The poor guy. Here I was locked in petty torment over my cast, struggling inwardly with every coach I'd ever disappointed, and Joe was ... who knows where? No place good. In fact, I knew very little about him. I didn't know that he had started guiding for the Fly Fisher's Place in 2009, that he'd done splendidly that year (the best in modern history for steelhead in the Deschutes), that he had suffered a depression in the fall after the season ended, that he'd been broke, that friends had found him work and loaned him money.

I didn't know that after his next guiding season, in 2010, he had gone into an even worse depression; that on December 26, 2010, he had written a suicide note and swallowed pills and taped a plastic bag over his head in the back offices of the Fly Fisher's Place; that he'd been interrupted in this attempt and rushed to a hospital in Bend; that afterward he had spent time in the psychiatric ward of the hospital; that his friends in Sisters and his boss, Jeff Perin, owner of the fly shop, had met with him regularly in the months following to help him recover.

I didn't know that after the next season, in late 2011, he had disappeared; that Perin, fearing a repetition, had called the state police; and that they had searched for him along the Deschutes Valley with a small plane and a boat, and eventually found him unharmed and returning home. Joe later told Perin he had indeed thought about killing himself during this episode but had decided not to.

I didn't know that Perin had refrained from firing Joe on several occasions—for example, when Joe was guiding an older angler who happened to be a psychiatrist with the apt name of Dr. George Mecouch, along with one of Dr. Mecouch's friends, and a repo man showed up with police officers and a flatbed, and they repossessed Joe's truck (a previous one), leaving Joe and his elderly clients stranded by the side of the road in the middle of nowhere at eleven o'clock at night. Dr. Mecouch, evidently an equable and humorous fellow, had laughed about the experience, thereby perhaps saving Joe's job. I did not know that Perin had permanently ended his professional relationship with Joe when Joe refused to guide on a busy Saturday in July of 2012 because he had received no tip from his clients of the day before.

The spot where Joe killed himself is out in the woods about six miles from Sisters. You drive on a rutted Forest Service road for the last mile or two until you get to a clearing with a large gravel pit and a smaller one beside it. Local people come here for target practice. Splintery, shot-up pieces of plywood lie on the ground, and at the nearer end the spent shotgun-shell casings resemble strewn confetti. Their colors are light blue, dark blue, pink, yellow, forest green, red, black, and purple. Small pools of muddy water occupy the centers of the gravel pits, and the gray, rutted earth holds a litter of broken clay-pigeon targets, some in high-visibility orange. At the clearing's border, dark pine trees rise all around.

Probably to forestall the chance that he would be interrupted this time, Joe had told some friends that he was going to Spokane to look for work, others that he would be visiting his children in California. On November 4, 2012, he spent the afternoon at Bronco Billy's, a restaurant-bar in Sisters, watching a football game and drinking Maker's Mark with beer chasers. At about six in the evening he left, walking out on a bar tab of about $18. The bartender thought he had gone outside to take a phone call. At some time after that, he drove to the gravel pit, parked at its northwest edge, and ran a garden hose from the exhaust pipe to the right rear passenger-side window, sealing the gaps around the pipe and in the window with towels and clothes. A man who went to the gravel pit to shoot discovered the body on November 14. In two weeks, Joe would have been forty-nine years old.

He left no suicide note, but he did provide a couple of visual commentaries at the scene for those who could decode them. The garden hose he used came from the Fly Fisher's Place. Joe stole it for this purpose, one can surmise, as a cry for help or a gesture of anger directed at his former boss, Jeff Perin.

Over the summer, Joe's weeks of illegal guiding had caught up with him when the state police presented him with a ticket for the violation. He would be required to go to court, and in all likelihood his local guiding career would be through, at least for a good while. Joe thought Perin had turned him in to the authorities; and in fact, Perin and other guides had done exactly that. Joe was often aggressive and contentious on the river, he competed for clients, and his illegal status made people even more irate. But, in the end, to say that Joe's legal difficulties were what undid him would be a stretch, given his history.

Joe's friend Diane Daviscourt, when she visited the scene, found an empty Marlboro pack stuck in a brittlebrush bush next to where Joe had parked. The pack rested upright among the branches, where it could only have been put deliberately. She took it as a sign of his having given up on everything, and as his way of saying, "Don't forget me."

John Hazel, the Deschutes River's senior guide, said Joe was a charismatic fellow who took fishing too seriously. "I used to tell him, 'It's only fishing, Joe.' He got really down on himself when he didn't catch fish. Most guides are arrogant—Joe possessed the opposite of that. Whoever he was guiding, he looked at the person and tried to figure out what that person wanted." Daviscourt, who had briefly been Joe's girlfriend, said he was her best friend, and made a much better friend than a boyfriend. "He fooled us all," she said. "I haven't picked up a fly-fishing rod since he died."

She made a wooden cross for him and put it up next to where she found the Marlboro pack. The cross says Joe R. on it in black marker, and attached to it with pushpins is a laminated photo of Joe, completely happy, standing in the river with a steelhead in his hands and a spey rod by his feet. On the pine needles beside the cross is a bottle of Trumer Pils, the brand Joe drank when she was buying.

Just before Joe died, J. T. Barnes was calling him a lot, partly to say hi, and partly because Joe had never paid him for helping on the trip with me. (He did split the tip, however.) For someone now out $600, J.T. had only kind words for Joe. "He was like the ideal older brother. And he could be so up, so crazy enthusiastic, about ordinary stuff. One day we were packing his drift boat before a trip, drinking beer, and I told him that I play the banjo. Joe got this astonished, happy look on his face, and he said, 'You play the banjo? No way! That is so great—I sing!' That made me laugh, but he was totally being serious. I play the banjo, Joe sings!"

Joe had six dollars in his wallet when he died. Kay, his sister, who lives in Napa, thought Joe's chronic lack of money was why he lost touch with his family. "Joe was always making bad decisions financially. Maybe, because he had a lot of pride, that made him never want to see us. But he was doing what he loved, supporting himself as a famous fishing guide. He had no idea how proud his family was of him."

Alex Gonsiewski, a highly regarded young guide on the river who works for John Hazel, said that Joe taught him most of what he knows. When Gonsiewski took his first try at running rapids that have drowned people, Joe was in the bow of the drift boat helping him through. "It's tough to be the kind of person who lives for extreme things, like Joe was," Gonsiewski said. "His eyes always looked sad. He loved this river more than anywhere. And better than anybody, he could dial you in on how to fish it. He showed me the river, and now every place on the river makes me think of him. He was an ordinary, everyday guy who was also amazing. I miss him every day."

The paths along the river that have been made by anglers' feet are well worn and wide. Many who come to fish the Deschutes are driven by a deep, almost desperate need. So much of the world is bullshit. This river is not. Among the many natural glories of the Northwest that have been lost, this valley—still mostly undeveloped, except for the train tracks—and its beautiful, tough fish have survived.

Joe was the nakedest angler I've ever known. He came to the river from a world of bullshit, interior and otherwise, and found here a place and a sport to which his own particular sensors were perfectly attuned. Everything was okay when he was on the river … Except that then everything had to stay that way continuously, or else horrible feelings of withdrawal would creep in. For me the starkest sadness about Joe's death was that the river and the steelhead weren't enough.

At the end of my float trip with Joe, just before we reached the river's mouth, he stopped at a nondescript, wide, shallow stretch with a turquoise-flowing groove. He said he called this spot Mariano, after Mariano Rivera, the Yankees' great relief pitcher, because of all the trips it had saved. I stood and cast to the groove just as told to, and a sudden river quake bent the spey rod double. The ten-pound steelhead I landed after a long fight writhed like a constrictor when I tried to hold it for a photograph.

The next evening, not long before I left for the airport, Joe and I floated the river above Maupin a last time. Now he wasn't my guide; he had me go first and fish a hundred yards or so ahead of him. Dusk deepened, and suddenly I was casting well again. I looked back at Joe, and he raised his fist in the air approvingly. At the end of his silhouetted arm, the glow of a cigarette could be seen. I rolled out one cast after the next. It's hard to teach a longtime angler anything, but Joe had taught me. He knocked the rust off my fishing life and gave me a skill that brought back the delight of learning, like the day I first learned to ride a bicycle. I remembered that morning when we were floating downstream among the crane flies in the sunlight. Just to know it's possible to be that happy is worth something, even if the feeling doesn't last. Hanging out with Joe uncovered long-overgrown paths back to childhood. Peace to his soul.

Reflections from the Pools

DAVID ADAMS RICHARDS

A letter to Anton

I HAVE TAKEN a trip with your mom down the Bartibog River after trout. It is in the late spring and the water is high. I could write about this, I suppose, and tell you how we found a small run below a pool called Toomey's Quarry, where, as my Green Butt Butterfly went across the water and disappeared, a trout came up and grabbed it and a bear appeared just above us, watching. I had to play that fish with an audience I was hoping did not disapprove.

That was long ago, thirty-eight years ago now, and that is one of the few things I remember about that particular trip, except the wind came up and it was colder as the day went on, and the rocks burdened us so much Peg said she would never run Bartibog again. She had packed a little lunch, and had brought napkins and white wine and wore a nice hat. Was it that trip or another where I cut my leg? No, Anton, that was another trip, the day I had walked down the long hill to Aggens Pool on the lower part of Bartibog River and fell on a glass bottle that lay off to the side of the pathway— Aggens Pool, which the boys all called (and the girls, too) Maggie Aggens Hole. I tore the sleeve from my shirt and wrapped my leg up and continued on.

There is a song about Maggie Aggens Hole that comes from the age of your mom's uncles. It is sung to the Johnny Horton tune "The Battle of New Orleans." These were boys who lived and died along the Bartibog River and grew up to be as grand as any men you might meet. One who came back shell-shocked from Italy (that horrendous forgotten part of the Second World War) and saved money so he could pay for his own funeral because Veterans Affairs would not; that is, they cut his pension, and he was left alone and broke. Oh yes, it seems to me that's a part of fishing rivers as well, for he haunted the rivers that I, too, remember as part of my past, a past drifting away like a solitary fisherman poling a Nor West canoe down the Miramichi River at twilight.

Some nights you would see him walking home after dark, a string of trout from those hidden leaved-over pools deep in the Bartibog wood. In Bartibog I met the first real true fishermen, and went to Aggens Pool many times alone. It is one of the most beautiful trout pools in the whole Miramichi Valley, and here's a secret: it doesn't always produce, but when it does, there are magnificent moments, clandestine, for in some way all great fishing is a secretive act—an act between you and God. Don't laugh at your old man, Anton, for when the fish takes, you will know I tell the truth. There are brook-run sea trout weighing upward of five or six pounds, and salmon migrate there in the fall, move upriver under the leaves turning golden in the frost, and lay silent in the cold water of Kennan or Green Brook Pool, or any of the other pools that have formed our Bartibog River. Eagles will soar in the blue sky, the feathers at the tips of their wings moving just slightly in the currents of air far, far above us. If it is early enough in the day, the sun will light off the ice-covered boulders and seem like fire through the alders, the wind will only blow a little, and you might see a buck in rut against the morning slopes, or a bear meandering away into its den for winter. Anton, I know you might think that fall is a strange time to fish, but when the sun does its job and warms those boulders, the fish begin to move and a bright patterned fly will work. I have seen men take a fishing rod, some butt bugs, and flies and, packing a shotgun in their canoe, pole down the river from the Bailey Bridge that crosses the river near the highway, to Green Brook Pool, and onward to Kennan Pool and Toomey's Quarry, watching for partridge on the wooded slopes, for salmon moving up the winding rocky river just at dusk.

I fell out of the canoe that day with Peg, that day in springtime so long ago that I look upon us as children now. You see it was growing late and I had managed to take a few trout, and Peg had picked a bag of fiddleheads on the warm riverbanks at midday, moving from patch to patch through the spring grass, like women have done for hundreds of years. Later we moved downriver with the sun in our eyes. I began to look around her to see how the water was bundling to rapids below us. Night was coming on, and we had another four miles to our old car.

"Where is it?" I finally said.

"Where is what?" Peg asked.

"You know, that rock."

"What rock—everywhere I look I see rocks—there is not a place on the whole Bartibog River I don't see rocks."

So I stood in the stern, to see where the hidden boulder was, that boulder just below the gravel-pit pool—everyone who has ever been in a canoe will know the one I mean. But when I stood, I saw, alas, we were right upon it. Son, I went flying into the air over your mom's head and into the water, with a kind of embarrassing *ker-splash*. Shadows played across the water in the late day, and I had to take off my clothes and dry them out on the rocks of the riverbank.

There is a poem by the great Newfoundland romantic bard Al Pittman called "Once When I Was Drowning."

I almost drowned trying to cross the Northwest Miramichi River later that same June. I went down in my chest waders just above Little River Pool, a magnificent pool on the main Norwest Miramichi where I took a twelve-pound salmon in late June that year. The water was still high at that crossing and I felt my legs go out from under me when I became tangled up in rapids. I tried desperately to keep my balance, but you know me on my feet—I had no luck. Down I went in my chest waders. The pressure from water rushing into my waders caused my body to turn in complete circles under the surface, my feet bobbing. But I shoved my arms against the river bottom and managed to right myself, and then swim across to the shore, my waders weighing an extra seventy pounds and my rod in my left hand. (I was alone at the time and this was an incident I was not going to tell anyone, but it is something that has happened to so many of us not telling you seems silly; besides, I am not bothered by my own silliness anymore.) I took off my waders, walked down to the little river pool, and on my fourth cast hooked a grilse. But the fish jumped three times and spit the hook.

I was lost in the woods half a dozen times, once trying to find a better way into Cedar Pool on the Norwest Miramichi back in 1982.

Cedar Pool was such a grand pool back then that a dedicated fisherman would do almost anything to get to it (the winter years have changed it, and now it is not as good). There are rapids flooding over boulders at the top, very heavy water in spring, and it's hard to cross to where one must fish from the other side, but salmon lay from the rip that is about midpoint of the pool down to where the large flat rock sits just near the bottom end.

Your godfather Peter McGrath and I decided to cut straight through the woods from his camp, and got so completely turned around, so totally bamboozled, that we finally had to do something unusual: we had to look at our compass, and came to realize we were going in the one direction we did not believe we were going in, a direction away from both the great Norwest river and an old nineteenth-century logging road we had walked along just a half an hour before. Once we realized our mistake, we were back on the logging road we had left within ten minutes.

We tented on the rivers of my youth—that is, the south branch of the Sevogle and the Norwest Miramichi many times—in June or July back in those days, fishing for salmon. Your mom's cousin David Savage and I ran Green Brook, that fertile brook cut out in the Bartibog wilderness that runs down to Green Brook Pool on the Bartibog, a half mile above the Bathurst highway; ran the Norwest and the Little Souwest Miramichi, took fish (trout and salmon) on all those rivers, twenty to thirty years ago now. And along Renous River and the main Souwest Miramichi as well. I fished the conjunction of three great rivers, called Square Forks, perhaps one of the most pristine fishing areas in the world. I am proud of that. And I am proud, too, of releasing more fish there than I ever kept.

On the Norwest Miramichi, Peter and I ran a canoe at least once a year from the Elbow stretch to the village of Wayerton, a distance of about fifteen miles, the great water teaming with young salmon—grilse—moving up, following the big salmon in. We would camp halfway down, make up a fire on the beach, drink our tea, listen to the water in the darkness, and now and then look up at the stars. We would beat that water to death for fish. Years before us, a friend of your grandfather told me, he would run the same stretch of river at the same time of year. He and his brother would pole down in a ragged old canoe, hook into a dozen salmon and huge sea-run trout, and never meet another soul. That was an age before Peter and David and me, and as you know, our day is now an age ago.

I will also let you in on a secret. There are very few people I would trust with my life. David Savage and Peter McGrath are two.

The Norwest Miramichi was the river where I learned to read a pool and to know the hot spots in it. I took my first salmon from that branch, strangely enough with the first cast I ever made. That was far above Cedar Pool and far above the Elbow stretch as well—miles of wilderness, of rushing water and jagged hills. We traveled on woods roads so overgrown that branches would snap the truck mirrors off, or at times punch a light out.

That seemed all a part of it back then. So, much of the hilarity of our youth was not spent in vain.

It was June 22, over forty years ago. We were at Brandy Landing Pool—B&L, as it is known to Miramichiers.

I cast my first cast. Not a very good cast, either, but I felt my line tighten instantly. I was using a Red Butt Butterfly, number 6, with stiff wings. I had in my hands my first nine-and-a-half-foot Fenwick rod. The rapids at the top of B&L Pool broaden out into dark, deep water where fish rest after their journey up the Stony Brook stretch of the Norwest Miramichi, but my first cast was right into those turbulent rapids at the very top of the pool, so that particular fish must have been moving through. It was a male grilse; that is, a small salmon, about four pounds. I did not foul-hook him—he took hard.

The next spring, June 4, I took two large salmon and five large trout one evening at that same pool, standing only a few yards down from where I made my first cast the year before. The sea-run trout had come in amid the big salmon, and Peter and I were lucky enough to find them. Peter caught five trout that evening as well.

B&L Pool is at the top part of the Stony Brook stretch, in the deepest and most rugged part of the Norwest Miramichi Valley. It is a long bank to climb up or down, a hard pool to get to, and as I write this, it is many miles away. But we went there in late spring and early summer for almost twenty years, listening to the water roar beneath us as we walked over the long, sweetly shaded hill, meeting very few other fishermen. Anton, I will tell you—I guess I have been as content there as any place I have ever been.

The woods have drawn me since I was a boy, and in many ways when I am there I am a boy still. I can sit for hours in the shade of elms and birch. I watch others fish. And I am just as content as if I was fishing. At one time lots of things mattered to me that do not matter much anymore. Son, I have had enough fame to know it is a lie. And except for being with my family, I am most content when I am by myself. The woods and waterways of the Miramichi have kept me alive.

I told my brother this past June that I now understood why our uncle Richard went into the woods as a boy of twelve and remained a woodsman all of his life, appearing at the doorway of my grandmother's house at ten at night, coming out from some solitary camp way up on the river and then being gone before breakfast the next morning, coming out again three weeks later.

He had much work to do.

Richard Adams was a salmon guide on the Matapedia. And many say he became the greatest salmon guide of his generation, guiding presidents and movie stars. He carried Farrah Fawcett on his back across a river, guided Jimmy and Rosalynn Carter. Sometimes I get letters from people as far away as Pennsylvania asking me to tell them of my many memories of fishing with him. I would gladly do so, but I never did fish with him. The memory I have is that one day he carried me down to the Matapedia River and put me into his twenty-six-foot Restigouche canoe to have my picture taken when I was four years old. He never drove a car; he never had his own house. He would hitchhike wherever he went. He told people who bothered to ask that he had heard that I was a writer of some merit, though he did not know much about me. But one day not long before he died, someone I know visited his place to do an interview and spied three piles of news clippings. When Richard left the room, the fellow took a glance at them. One pile contained stories on the Atlantic salmon; the second, stories written about Richard Adams. The third pile was stories he had collected over the years about me.

Three years ago, a man from Boston sent me Richard's picture, his face chiseled out as if from granite, the shock of white hair to his shoulder, the old hat that had become emblematic of his life.

I have deep respect for the best guides.

An old guide visited Peter and me, once, years ago, after we ran an upper stretch of the Norwest Miramichi River called the North Pole branch, searching for trout. He came in to sit in our camp at night and we bragged to him about having come down that hard run all the way from Lizard Brook, having poled the canoe across flats and through rapids. He spit his snuff into the fire and nodded. Then he commented shyly and politely:

"But youse see—the best thing for youse to do is pole yer canoe upriver nine or ten mile beyond that brook. That's where the trouts really is. When I was a boy, I would pole up there against the rapids and find the fish. I would camp out fer days up there. I had an old rod and some three or four flies. Some trout up there went seven pounds."

You can imagine we did not think our own journey so exceptional after that.

The very next year—I think I was twenty-seven or twenty-eight—I walked three miles of river in my bare feet because I had torn my sneakers apart on the rocks. So both my feet were cut, but not as badly as one might think. Late that evening, just before I got to my truck, Peter managed to take one fish far below a pool called Moose Brook on the Depot stretch of the Norwest Miramichi River, above the Stony Brook stretch. That was the year I began to fish Brown Bug with Orange Hackle, and it became my favorite fly, for I knew fish would show for it even if they did not take. Besides, I was never a great caster and a Bug seemed to compensate for that fact.

And then I could tell you this.

For almost fifteen years I had a dog named Roo. Well, Roo traveled in my truck, shared my adventures and my baloney sandwiches, drank pop out of my cap, licked my face whenever I caught a fish, sat on the rocky banks as I fished a pool, lay down on the supplies in the middle of the canoe when we ran the river. At times in those years she was as close to me as any person, my only companion along the distant rivers, and except for my wife and kids, I loved her most. Where I *needed* her most was on the south branch of the Sevogle River when I fished it alone. Down over those great spruce hills one is in solitude, and there are many days you might not see another soul.

It is a place of retreat, wilderness, where the fishing is best in late July and the blackflies are ferocious. Three Minute Pool, Disappointment Pool, Island Pool, White Birch, Teacup, Milk Jug... I have been fortunate to take fish from them all. And by "fish" I mean salmon.

The best thing about the South branch is that you don't need waders; the water is warm enough to fish in sneakers and jeans (though still cool enough that the fish are active). It makes traveling over the slippery boulders easier. And so you can wander along its harsh and slippery banks unencumbered. If I traveled a long way from where we parked and it was late in the day, I would simply say "Truck," and

Roo would turn and go, leading me back up the narrow pathways to the overgrown road, stopping to patiently wait until I caught up. I know I would not have made it back without her. Even when she had arthritis, she would hobble with me down to those tea-colored pools of mornings long ago. Yes, she is gone now, but somehow still with me when I think of her.

This past June I spent a night showing your brother John how to tie a blood knot. I used to tie them quite a bit when I used a tapered leader. It is a valuable knot for him to know, just in case he wants to lengthen his leader and I'm not around. We are going in to the Stony Brook stretch with my older brother for two days. The water will be high now, and I know it will be hard fishing. It has been raining intermittently for a week or so, and I have watched it from our old farmhouse near the mouth of the Bartibog. Each day the clouds seem lower in the nor'west sky, and the trees toss in the wind.

I am hoping John will catch his first salmon somewhere along the Stony Brook run. I am hoping that this is the year. He grew up in Toronto, and has been to the water only three or four times. Two years ago we ran the Norwest Miramichi River on a day in early July and I hooked four fish but he had no luck. I handed him the rod so he could feel in his arms how beautiful and powerful and majestic a salmon is.

So, Anton, your brother arrived from our house in Fredericton the day before. I took him to the Bartibog, and we went to Aggens Pool. The water was high there, and no fish would take. In fact, he could hardly walk in his waders far enough out to cast a line. I remembered the trip where I had cut my leg. I was then almost exactly the same age as he was that day, and it was only a week from the same day of the year.

"How many trout did you catch?" John asked, after we fished for three hours without seeing even a small fish roll.

"I caught seven that morning," I said. "All nice trout—but you will have your day—you will have many days," I said. Well, I hoped and prayed that might be true. But the road to Aggens Pool is now a harder road down and we need a four-wheel drive to get in. A beaver pond has flooded the very path where I fell and cut my leg open, and a four-wheeler track, something unheard of when I was John's age, cuts through to the pool from the right side. Poaching is rampant on the river now, Anton—trolling for fish at the mouth, nets strung across pools far upriver where wardens almost never venture. And bass are in the river, in ever-larger schools.

That night it was still raining hard, down against the raspberry bushes, and the clouds were dark. There was a smell of lilac in the wind, and the grass was green all down the four acres that we own here.

The two water barrels at the side of the house were full, and now and again lightning would flash almost splendidly against the far-off pines, and thunder rumble far across the great Miramichi Bay.

So I painfully showed him the knot. Still, John catches on to things. He is a good mechanic and a great carpenter. He was tying blood knots as good as or better than I was in an hour.

"Like this?" he asks.

The next morning the storm had rolled away, and we went in my brother's jeep, and the road into Stony was different—you know, I simply forgot how long a way it was—and there was a new camp from the last time I was there, oh such a long, long time ago now. But taking one look at the water, I felt it was too high yet. I knew there would be fish here, but I thought, "They will be moving through—resting farther up toward B&L Pool."

That did not mean we couldn't hook one. But after the first day we had not. We fished the home pool, and crossed the river in high water and went down to the pool below. The wind always comes up the valley after one o'clock and makes it very hard to cast—especially for John, who is just learning (but he is doing better and better each day). John has heard so much about the Stony Brook stretch over the years, during those winter days in Toronto with its sound of buses and subways, I was hoping for even one fish to show. But the great Miramichi River can break your heart, and yes, it often does.

We crossed the river again, and late in the day, after supper, went to the pool above the camp. It is a beautiful pool that bends left over big rocks and you cast into the long, deep run that results. But it was roaring water—hard to work your fly when your line is carried so swiftly and straightens too soon. The wind had died, as it always does in the evening, and two deer came out to munch at clover upriver by a hundred yards.

Finally we decided to call it a day.

I was using a wading stick given to me by Dr. Cole, a fishing pal from days gone by, when I fished the great Square Forks, and I certainly needed it to cross back in the heavy current just at dark. John and my brother Bill managed to cross on their own. Anton, you know they have better balance than I.

Still, nothing to show for all that but a small trout.

I told John there would be fish tomorrow.

We woke early.

I did not fish that day. It does not matter to me now. You see, sometimes, if you are very lucky, you realize that very little matters except those you love. In fact, nothing else. I am less inclined to rush toward the water, knowing it will always be there when I get to it. And the wind was hard, blowing the water into a kind of endless chop; the sky was dull and gray and then brightened. I went up along the road, collected some firewood, brewed tea for lunch, and boiled a piece of grilse we had from last year.

I walked through the woods to each pool, looking down into them with my Polaroid sunglasses, trying to see fish moving, but I could not tell in the wind. I know friends of mine like David and Peter probably could. So I sat out in the sun and ate my lunch, drank black tea. I watched a chipmunk chatter, its tail in the air, and said hello to a birch partridge who swore at me up and down while trying to protect her three chicks. About four in the afternoon my brother saw fish moving up beyond the home pool. But they weren't stopping.

He and my son worked every pool again—all day. The water had dropped, but not enough.

Another two days, I thought, as we sat out at the fire that night—then it will be great fishing. But we had only one morning left.

That night the stars came out and I remembered running the river with Peter thirty years before, stopping halfway down to pitch a tent.

So I thought about what to do, and I said the only pool to go to was B&L. The last pool up on the Stony Brook stretch, a hard pool to get to still. Especially hard from this side of the river.

Bill hesitated, and finally said he did not want me to go.

"I would prefer you not go," he said. I knew that was coming, Anton. Maybe you knew it too. I guess I had been waiting for it all year in one way or another. From this side of the river, we would have to go over the bank on the far side of the pool, a horrendous climb, and then cross the river above the falls. It was the long vertical climb back up that worried Bill. The problem—well, it was not a problem to me, but to your uncle Bill—was the two heart attacks I had in the last year. It is not something I worry much about, and I do not want you to ever worry about it for my sake. Still, Bill did. I knew he would say this, so I drank my tea in silence and looked up at the stars, coming out now in the brilliant night.

"It's my heart," I said. "And it feels pretty sound—and if I do die, I will die at B&L. What better place on the whole Miramichi could I find?"

"I'm not having it," Bill said. "David, we're forty miles from anywhere."

I told him it was a foolish worry, that I could make that climb. But he would not give in.

"If you don't want us to go, we won't," John said.

I shrugged, spit the last of my tea into the fire. "Don't be so damn foolish," I said. "What does it matter besides you having a chance at a fish? Bill and I both want that—but watch how you cross that river; don't go down in your waders there!"

The next morning, I woke John and handed him one of my boxes of flies. "Look through them," I said. "Take that Green Machine that Dave Savage tied me. It will work up there—you will see fish."

That day, of all days, they forgot the camera on the camp porch. I ran up the road to give it to them, but they had gone. I did not hear the truck again for almost four hours.

Anton, I want to tell you something: crossing the river at B&L is not too tough most of the time, but in high water it can be. When you cross a river, it is always the boulders you does not see that will tangle you. Sometimes they are right in front of you, but the swirl below you is at times as black as tar, capped by white spray rushing by. So I wondered if the crossing would be easy or tough. This is what I thought of while I sat there. I knew every inch of that pool, too, and wondered how they would fish it—where John would step into it, and how he would work his way down.

Then I went for a walk back upriver. I ate my lunch staring at the water, and smelled smoke from a forest fire I hoped (and actually prayed) was not close.

But all things work out. I give you my word. Now, I did not see my oldest boy catch his first fish. But he caught it using a Green Machine our friend Dave Savage had tied. John crossed the river of my youth at the same age I had, and fished the same pool. But it wasn't that pool where he got the fish. It was the run 250 yards below the pool—a run my friend and your godfather, and one of the finest of woodsmen, Peter McGrath, had discovered back in those early days years ago. The run we would fish once a day for three weeks every year. My brother had told John to go and try it. So John walked down to it. He put on a new leader and tied a blood knot. He stepped into the water, and waded halfway across the river before he cast. And he was beginning to cast well. On the fourth cast, Anton, his line tightened, and a young salmon, the same size as the fish I caught forty years ago, almost to the day, jumped high in the splendid morning air.

"Bill!" he called. "I'm not sure, but I think I have a fish on."

And so he had.

Anyway, we drove home later. It was mild. There was the smell from a fire in Quebec, a hazy smoke all across the river where I have spent so much of my life. Peg was at the door, smiling like that girl who ran the Bartibog with me thirty-eight years ago.

Your mom's gentle smile made me realize that all things are possible. My son, there is nothing ever to fear.

I will get to B&L again. Roo and I will clamber down the banks of the great river together. Me with a rod in my hand, she stopping to wait as we make our way.

I believe that's the way it will be.

Someday, soon.

Contributors

MARNI JACKSON is the author of several nonfiction books and the former Rogers Chair of the Literary Journalism program at the Banff Centre, where she is on the faculty of the Mountain and Wilderness Writing program. She has won numerous awards for her journalism and has a collection of short fiction in the works.

THOMAS MCGUANE is an American novelist and screenwriter, well known for both his cowboy lifestyle in Montana and his precise, risky writing style. His apocalyptic novel *92 in the Shade,* about a Key West fishing guide, was made into a cult film starring Peter Fonda, and his nonfiction essay collection *The Longest Silence* is often recommended as one of the finest books ever written about fishing.

CHARLES WILKINS is the author of fifteen books, including the memoirs *The Circus at the Edge of the Earth,* about his travels with the Great Wallenda Circus, and *In the Land of Long Fingernails,* about a summer he spent working in a large Toronto cemetery. His latest book, *Little Ship of Fools,* chronicles his recent journey across the Atlantic Ocean in a rowboat.

IAN PEARSON is a veteran Toronto writer, editor, and radio producer. He has worked as an editor at *Maclean's* and *Toronto* magazine. His articles have appeared in most major Canadian magazines, winning five National Magazine Award nominations. He was books producer for CBC Radio's *Morningside* and a contributing editor of *Saturday Night* magazine during the 1990s. He was a long-serving editor at the Banff Centre and is a lifelong fly fisherman.

KENNETH KIDD is a veteran newspaperman whose work has appeared in the *Globe and Mail* and the *Toronto Star,* where he was a long-serving feature writer. He has won National Newspaper and National Magazine awards. His book *Crucible of Flames,* co-written with Jim Coyle, covers the 1812 war between Canada and the United States.

CHARLES GAINES was born and raised in the American south, went on to study writing at the University of Iowa, and, during the 1970s, wrote *Stay Hungry* and *Pumping Iron,* on the subculture of bodybuilding. (Both were made into films starring a young Arnold Schwarzenegger.) In 1995, he published the autobiographical novel *A Family Place*, which documented the building of a family cabin in Nova Scotia. *The Next Valley Over: An Angler's Progress* (2001) details his fly-fishing experiences all over the world. Gaines also co-invented paintball, a stalking game loosely based on the 1924 short story by Richard Connell, "The Most Dangerous Game."

JAKE MACDONALD is a Canadian author who has produced twelve books of both fiction and nonfiction, and hundreds of stories for assorted journals and magazines. Many of the articles and books have won awards. His latest novel, *Jordan River*, will soon be published.

DAVID CARPENTER lives in Saskatoon, and is the author of numerous novels, essays, short stories, and books of nonfiction. His stage is the great plains of Saskatchewan, and his characters are the unique and colorful people who live there. His latest work, *A Hunter's Confession*, explores the history of hunting and its place in our culture. Among his many interests are fly rods and the banjo.

ANNIE PROULX is an author of French Canadian and New England parentage who studied for an MA in Montreal and went on to contribute stories to science fiction digests and fishing and hunting magazines (in which she sometimes published under the name E. A. Proulx to avoid gender bias).

Her books and awards are too numerous to summarize, but her second novel, *The Shipping News* (1993), won the Pulitzer Prize for Fiction and her lyrical short story "Brokeback Mountain," first published in *The New Yorker*, was adapted into a critically praised motion picture. John Updike selected her short story "The Half-Skinned Steer" for inclusion in *The Best American Short Stories of the Century*.

WAYNE CURTIS was born and raised in New Brunswick and caught his first big salmon at age eight. He worked as a river guide, and became a writer in the early 1970s. He has written sixteen books and dozens of articles and short stories about his beloved Miramichi River. His last book, *Of Earthly and River Things: An Angler's Memoir*, was published by Goose Lane Editions.

IAN FRAZIER grew up in Ohio and attended Harvard University, where he was on the staff of the *Harvard Lampoon*. He is now one of the most popular contributors to *The New Yorker*, sketching sharply observant and comic depictions of life on the fringes of American society. In nonfiction works such as *Great Plains, Family,* and *On the Rez*, Frazier combines first-person narrative with in-depth research on topics that include Native Americans, fishing, and the outdoors.

DAVID ADAMS RICHARDS is a well-known Canadian writer and devoted fly fisherman who has produced twelve novels and two books of nonfiction. The Miramichi region of

New Brunswick and the rural lives of its inhabitants are central to his fiction. He has won many awards and is one of few writers to win the Governor General's Award for both a novel (*Nights below Station Street*) and a memoir (*Lines on the Water*).